Building a Family

A Handbook for Parenting with God

Building a Family

A Handbook for Parenting with God

Marilyn Spaw Krock

PAULIST PRESS
New York/Mahwah, N.J.

Four lines from the song "When You Tell One Lie, It Leads to Another" from the *Standing Tall* series by Janeen Brady, copyright © Brita Music Inc., 1981. Used by permission of the author.

The Scripture quotations contained herein are from the New Revised Standard Version Bible, copyright © 1989 by the Division of Christian Education of the National Council of the Churches of Christ in the U.S.A., and are used by permission. All rights reserved.

Cover and interior design by Lynn Else

Library of Congress Cataloging-in-Publication Data

    Krock, Marilyn Spaw
    Building a family : a handbook for parenting with God / Marilyn Spaw Krock.
       p. cm.
    Includes bibliographical references.
    ISBN 0-8091-4102-7
    1. Parents—Religious life. 2. Parenting—Religious aspects—Christianity. I. Title.
    BV4529 .K76 2002
    248.8′45—dc21

2002007619

Published by Paulist Press
997 Macarthur Boulevard
Mahwah, New Jersey 07430

www.paulistpress.com

Printed and bound in the
United States of America

Contents

Introduction—TIME = LOVE 1
- TIME—A Critical Family Element 2
- Quality vs. Quantity Debate 3
- TIME Slips Away 5

Section 1—Making TIME to Develop Relationships

Chapter 1—Trust 9
- Developing Trust During Childhood 9
- Trust Encourages Teens 13
- In God We Trust 14

Chapter 2—Individuality 17
- Appreciating Unique Personalities 17
- Learning Styles Differ 18
- Family Constellation—Always Unique 19

Chapter 3—Mealtimes 23
- Sacredness of Mealtime 23
- Avoiding Mealtime Conflict 25
- Heritage of Family Meals 27

Chapter 4—Enthusiasm 30
- "En Theos"—In the Spirit of God 30
- Watching for Miracles 31
- Taking Care of #1 33

Section 2—Making TIME to Appreciate Family History

Chapter 5—Traditions 39
- Appreciating "Roots" 39
- Creating New Traditions 40
- Religious Traditions Essential 42

Contents

Chapter 6—Inheritance 45

- How YOU Were Parented .45
- Genetics Plays Important Role 47
- Economic Expectations 49

Chapter 7—Memories 53

- What Is Remembered? 53
- Creating Memories 55
- Keeping Memories Alive 56

Chapter 8—Enjoyment 59

- TIME—Children's Best Reward 59
- Keep a Sense of Humor 61
- Laughing *with*, Not *at* 62

Section 3—Making TIME for Communication

Chapter 9—Talking and Listening 67

- Reflective Listening 67
- Finding the Words 68
- Problem-Solving Skills 70

Chapter 10—Interaction 72

- Conflict Resolution 72
- Family Meetings 74
- Television Affects Interaction .76

Chapter 11—Management 80

- TIME Management Skills 80
- Using TIME Wisely 82
- Financial Management 84

Chapter 12—Encouragement 87

- Parents as Cheerleaders 87
- Creating Lovable/Capable Children 88
- Natural/Logical Consequences 91

Contents

Section 4—Making TIME to Develop Parenting Skills

Chapter 13—**T**ogetherness 97
  • Agree On Parenting Techniques 97
  • Communication Is Key 98
  • Remember Why You Two Married 99

Chapter 14—**I**ntimacy 102
  • Parents as Sexual Role Models 102
  • Parental Privacy Essential 103
  • Parents as Sexuality Educators 106

Chapter 15—**M**orality 110
  • Role Models of Values 110
  • Development of Conscience 112
  • Respect for Others 114

Chapter 16—**E**valuation 118
  • Review Family Life 118
  • Use Educational Resources 119
  • Seek Professional Help 120

Section 5—Resources/Appendices

  Appendix 1—Resources Cited in Text 125

  Appendix 2—Web Sites for Resources/Catalogs 128

  Appendix 3—Suggestions for Parent Education 130

  Appendix 4—Parenting Handouts .134

Notes 153

Bibliography 155

Dedication

Grateful acknowledgment must be extended to my outstanding husband, helpmate, and source of strength, Lon. His calm patience, developed through years of being husband, father, and pediatrician, buoyed me up when trepidation over writing a book nearly paralyzed me.

Appreciation also goes to our three children—Kevin, Joseph, and Kristina—who continue to teach us the meaning of "parenting," plus furnish me with humorous anecdotes with which to lighten my message. Along with our wonderful "other daughters," Adrienne (Kevin's wife) and Eileen (Joe's wife), and our adorable grandsons, Matthew and Spencer (Kevin's sons), all have encouraged me to share the wisdom I am gaining as I journey through life.

During our journey God places people in our lives who inspire, nurture, and challenge us to grow. To my large extended family, many faithful longtime friends, coworkers at the Archdiocese of Los Angeles, and fellow parishioners at Holy Trinity Parish in San Pedro, thank you for sharing your lives, your faith experiences, and most of all your love.

Introduction

❧

TIME = LOVE

Psalms 127:3—
"[Children] are indeed a heritage from the Lord, the fruit of the womb a reward."

When my children were young, I thought I was pretty busy as a stay-at-home mother. There always seemed to be more to do than I had time to accomplish. My devoted husband, always helpful, had a pediatric practice to maintain, but we made time with our children a high priority. When I returned to school, and then became a working mother, I discovered how much busier I would have to be to keep everything functioning. Only then did I start realizing the extreme commitment my mother had made in raising me and my two brothers by herself, following my father's early death.

Looking back on those years, I marvel at how well she kept us all together, fed, clothed, and housed. Her organizational skills had to have been terrific. She worked from our home until my youngest brother was in school, then assumed a full-time secretarial position. How she made time for everything that needed to be done, and still had time to play with us and take us places, is the miracle of mothering. Because children equate time with love, we knew we were greatly loved.

Traveling through life and trying to be the best parent possible, I have availed myself of many educational opportunities. Some of the

1

most important lessons I have learned, however, came from my childhood and the loving ways in which I was parented. In composing this short handbook, I hope to share a variety of ideas gleaned from life and learning. Hopefully, many of the suggested activities are already incorporated into your parenting plan. Other hints on methods of creating, maintaining, and enriching your own happy, healthy family may stimulate further study. Parenting is the most important career to which persons can dedicate themselves. Studying to improve skills is essential to every career. Do not shortchange your family in such an important area. The results of *your* parenting will have a ripple effect for generations to come.

• TIME—A Critical Family Element

Everyone is gifted with twenty-four hours in a day. We each receive the very same 1,440 minutes every day of our lives. At the end of the day, do we reflect on all we have achieved or denigrate ourselves for not having accomplished more? There are so many demands on our time.

When we are parents, there is one extremely important fact we must keep in mind—to children TIME equals LOVE. The more time we spend with our children, the more love we show them. With our adult minds we know that this is not necessarily true. However, young children are only able to think *concretely*. What they *experience,* they understand.

Parents spend a lot of time at work, so children think their parents must really *love* work. Parents may spend time exercising every day; do they *love* that? Perhaps hobbies, socializing, or talking on the telephone with family and friends take up a good portion of parents' free time. Computers, the Internet, and television can sop up vast amounts of time. Do parents *love* these things more than they *love* their children? Probably not, but parents may not realize the messages that children are receiving from them.

How much time is dedicated to being with each child in a meaningful way every day? When was the last time you and your child sat together playing a board game, reading a book, working a puzzle, singing songs, giving a back rub, or listening attentively to one another? At the current pace of living, many people become "time frenzied." We all need to slow down for the sake of our own mental health, as well as the health of our families.

I still remember the day my four-year-old son (now an adult) said to me as the two of us were driving, "You don't REALLY listen. You just go uh-huh, uh-huh." He was right! My mind was somewhere else and his talk was background noise. Children know—so listen, respond appropriately, ask questions, and be interested.

Try to use travel time in the car as a bonding time with children. Talk with them about their dreams for the future, tell stories from your childhood, play "I Spy" games, make up silly songs. Please DO NOT make calls on your cellular phone, laughing and talking with friends, while your child sits ignored.

• Quality vs. Quantity Debate

Being engaged in parent education, I often hear parents say that they just cannot spend a quantity of time with their children, but the time they do spend together is real quality time. Parents cannot program time to be *quality*. It becomes one more chore on the "to do" list. Children are not made that way. When a parent finds a spot of time to dedicate to a child, the child may not be receptive to the plan. They may have plans of their own, especially if they are not used to spending quantity time with the parent.

The parent may in reality be interfering with the child's plan, which sets the parent up for failure.

Often "quality" activities go awry because parents, wanting desperately for the time together to be meaningful, over-plan and set unrealistic expectations on the outcome of the time shared. A long, exhausting day at an amusement park may turn into a tearful, stressful experience instead of the delightful, fun-filled excursion it was meant to be. Then parents become angry at the ingratitude of the child.

It is in the boredom of spending quantity time together that a parent and child may occasionally experience true quality time. Some of the most meaningful discussions I held with my three children when they were young occurred while driving one on one, running errands, going to and from sporting activities, or doing the school run. This becomes a good time to find out how their life is going. Some days they are talkative, other days they are not. You cannot, however, make a child talk. My daughter told me once that talking to me was like being "grilled."

Bedtime back rubs provided another excellent occasion for developing quality time. I started each evening with the youngest and worked my way up. They each had five minutes of my undivided attention, by their digital bedside clocks. Soon they learned that if we got a good discussion going I might just hang around longer. Even teenagers appreciate getting the kinks worked out of their neck and shoulders when they have been studying. Listening to the music they were playing often became a focus of discussion. They learned to change stations quickly when they saw me coming, knowing a discussion on lyrics could ensue.

Camping, for our family, still remains the best way to spend quantity time together, and from it we get a lot of genuine quality time. The absence of telephones (before cellular) has been the greatest asset, followed closely by the lack of television. Out of the "boredom," we play board games, sing songs, and tell stories around the campfire, and develop memories to last a lifetime.

Another surefire way to obtain some quantity time is to declare a "hooky" day. Get up one morning and surprise the family by calling in for a "personal day," let the children stay home from school, and spend the day together doing something, or doing nothing. Stay in pajamas and play board games. Fly kites at a park. Luckily, with year-round school in some areas, you will not look conspicuous having a picnic on a weekday. Start a tradition on the first day of spring or winter.

• TIME Slips Away

Television unconsciously can make us waste time, especially when turned on for just background noise. As you walk by you are captured and start watching a program you had no intention of viewing. If you want to see how much time is spent watching television, make a chart for one week and write down every time the television is on or off. It may be surprising.

Plan television viewing. On Sunday, review the television listing and write down which shows to watch, determining when the television will be allowed to be turned on. Be strong! Use a VCR to record worthwhile programs that come on at inconvenient times. Don't let yourself or your children become couch potatoes. Did you realize that you can bore children to bed when the television is not turned on after dinner?

Remember that watching television is not a child's right, it is a privilege. Children can earn television time by completing homework, chores, and reading. What they watch is of great importance. Monitor acceptable programs. Encourage educational shows that they might not choose on their own. Be aware of the amount of violence children are exposed to while watching television.

One other word of advice from the American Academy of Pediatrics: take television sets out of children's bedrooms! They do not have the maturity to control their viewing. Parents often have no idea what shows children are watching, or how late they stay up after parents go to bed.

Computers have become another area of concern because of material available over the Internet, the proliferation of violent games, and the addiction to e-mail and inappropriate chat rooms. Know what your children are doing. Keep computers in family areas for easier monitoring.

When answering machines became available, I fought it at first. Finally, being convinced that it helps with time control, I agreed to the purchase. My youngest child benefited the most as I could give her my undivided attention after dinner, until she was tucked into bed, without having to answer phone calls. Then, at my leisure, I could review messages and return calls as necessary. Just because the telephone is ringing, you do not have to answer it. In fact, it becomes very easy to turn off the ringer; just remember to turn it back on later. What a blessing!

Section 1

Making TIME to Develop Relationships

Chapter 1

Trust

Proverbs 3:5–6—
"Trust in the LORD with all your heart, / and do not rely on your own insight. / In all your ways acknowledge him and he will make straight your paths."

• Developing Trust During Childhood

Your child believes in you. In his eyes, you are strong, capable, powerful, and wise. Over time, he will demonstrate this trust by relaxing when you are near, coming to you with problems, and proudly pointing you out to others. Sometimes, he will also lean on you for protection from things that frighten him, including his own weaknesses. For example, in your presence he may try out new skills that he would never dare alone or with a stranger. He trusts you to keep him safe.[1]

Creating a trusting relationship with children during infancy is crucial to psychological development. Infants learn to trust not merely from having their basic needs met, but, more important, by the consistency and responsiveness with which those needs are met. The loving ways in which infants are handled, talked to, and cared for teach them in concrete ways that they can trust the world into which they have been so recently thrust.

Think how newborns must feel after being in "paradise" for nine months. They have been snug and secure, never experiencing cold, hunger, indigestion, or discomfort from dirty diapers. Is it any wonder that they cry?

Patience during an infant's adjustment period will prove invaluable as the months fly by and the baby becomes accustomed to the "outside world." Infants cannot be spoiled. They are simply trying to figure out who they are and what is happening to them. Parenting programs promoting adherence to strict schedules for infants have been found unacceptable by the American Academy of Pediatrics, some programs even verging on child abuse.

Trust normally develops first with the mother, but quickly extends to the father, as well as other relatives and caregivers who meet the infant's needs. Babies who have become trusting quickly adjust to life as a crawler and toddler. Trust is the anchor that allows infants, as they grow, to explore their world.

When separation anxiety starts occurring around eighteen months of age, children who have established a strong bond of trust adapt more quickly to the idea of parents' absences. (It still takes time and patience, however.) These children have learned that parents are trustworthy and will return.

Maintaining a child's trust requires honesty and reliability in keeping promises. When parents make promises to children, children believe that these promises will be kept. If a pattern of breaking promises develops, children lose trust in parents. Children who have not learned during childhood to trust other people have difficulty learning to trust others when they become adults.

Honesty is a value that must be taught to children from the early years. Trust works both ways—I trust you/you trust me. Learning that being honest and true to your word makes you an honorable person is essential. Parents' living example is the best teacher. When children see their parents telling "little white lies," the message becomes: sometimes lying is okay.

Do a quick check on your behavior. Do you return incorrect change to the cashier? Do you cheat on your child's age to pay lower admission prices? Do you reply to phone calls with, "Tell them I'm not home"? (Watch out. My young daughter once told a caller, "She says she's not home!")

Brite Music (see Appendix 1), a music program for children that teaches values, has a song about honesty:

When you tell one lie, it leads to another,
so you tell two lies to cover each other,
then you tell three lies, and, oh brother,
you're in trouble up to your ears![2]

Children must learn that telling lies can become a habit. Then a person is no longer trustworthy.

A word of caution: during the early years, magical thinking takes place and young children tell tales that might not be based in fact. This is different than intentional lying that develops when children are cognizant of what they are doing. Also, children sometimes hope to avoid punishment by not admitting to the truth. It is important for them to learn that by being honest they will be in less trouble than being caught in a lie.

Another aspect of honesty consists of being honest with children. In trying to spare children pain, adults often make up stories or refuse to tell children about things that are going on within the family, especially sickness, death, and divorce. Children hear things that are said and try to make sense of it in their own minds. Because of their limited understanding, they often create scenarios that are far worse than the reality. They take on guilt for what is happening due to lack of understanding situations. People often carry childhood guilt with them into adulthood.

When something is going on, include children by explaining, in developmentally appropriate ways, the circumstances and probable outcome. Even though the truth may be difficult for them to handle, children cope better when they are given information. They do not need all the details, just the basic facts, but be sure you have given them enough facts.

Etched forever in my mind is an experience I had when my boys were very young. Joseph, two years old, had been up all night screaming with an apparent earache. Only holding him to my chest in the rocking chair calmed him. In the morning, my husband got four-year-old Kevin dressed and fed and dropped him at preschool. Routine was disrupted. I told Kevin that Joey was sick, so I was going to take him to the doctor. I would be at preschool at pick-up time. Joey fell asleep in his car seat while returning from the doctor's office. Upon arriving at the preschool, I asked another mother to stand guard while I ran in to get Kevin—alone. Kevin looked up at me, his big blue eyes brimming with tears, and asked, "Did Joey die?" I'm sure he had worried about that all morning. It made me cry. I should have been more explicit in describing his brother's medical problem.

After learning that lesson, I tried to fill in more details as the children grew older, but that can also backfire. When I needed to go to the hospital for a minor surgical procedure, I told Joey, then five years old, that the part of Mommy where babies grow needed fixing; it was not any life-threatening problem; I would be home when he returned from school. He announced to the entire car pool that I was getting my "baby-maker" fixed! A year later his sister was born. I wonder how that affected his understanding of reproduction?

• Trust Encourages Teens

As children enter adolescence and the push for independence begins, trust remains an important issue. If parents have built strong bonds of trust in the earlier years, there is no reason to believe that trust should not continue. Let children know how important it is that you can trust each other. Explain how once trust is breached, reestablishing trust takes time and effort. Share examples from your life of happenings that destroyed your trust in someone.

Allow adolescents freedom within limits. As they prove they can handle that freedom, expand the limits, a little at a time. Help them practice making wise choices. A friend told me that when he was a teenager, his mother repeated, every time he left the house, "I know you will make the right choices!" That one phrase ruined a lot of his "potential fun" because he knew his mother trusted his good judgment.

In *Parenting Teenagers*, from Systematic Training for Effective Parenting [STEP], a respected program dealing with discipline issues, the following characteristics of a healthy parent-teen relationship are listed: mutual respect, mutual trust, mutual concern and caring, empathy, listening, participation in conflict resolution, and sharing thoughts and feelings.[3] The book details ways of achieving these lofty goals and enhancing the experience of parenting children through potentially tough times. The rewards for the effort are well worth the work involved.

I tell friends with young children to practice letting go a little at a time, giving freedom, expecting responsibility, imposing consequences. Once children have a driver's license, you begin to lose control. When they go away to college, you really lose control! Don't let young adults know this. We kept a sign in the family room that said, "Remember the Golden Rule: He who has the gold makes the rules!" Pray a lot and hope you have built a strong foundation.

One morning when my sixteen-year-old son had a day off from school, he parked his car blocking mine. In order to drive his sister to school, I took his car. On the way home my purse tipped over, spilling out the contents. Upon arriving home, I was gathering my things from under the seat when I found, to my stunned shock, a half bottle of rum! Let me tell you, I think I bodily lifted him out of his bed I was so angry, so disappointed, so hurt. He told me years later that seeing me crying and disillusioned was worse than any of the restrictions we imposed. Trusting him again took time.

• In God We Trust

Having established healthy, trusting relationships with other people throughout life, as we grow spiritually we find it easier to trust in the unconditional love of God. Persons who have not learned to trust people find trusting God especially difficult. Trust requires relinquishing control, believing that the "other" is looking out for our welfare. Often we turn things over to God for a while, but snatch problems back. Trusting and letting go takes a lifetime of practice.

Just as loving parents set limits and expect responsible behavior, so God guides us along life's journey. Unconditional love does not mean license to do whatever we please. Just as parents allow natural consequences to occur in order to help children learn, so must we accept the natural consequences of our behavior. God has given us guidelines for happy, healthy living. God sent his Son to share with us how we should live. Do we hear the messages? Have we learned any lessons? Establishing a trusting relationship with God helps us feel God's presence, perceive the nudging, and hear the whispers. We are in God's care. That love is unconditional!

When I was diagnosed with breast cancer, people would say, "How could God do this to you?" My reply was that God had not "done" this to me. My body did it to me, or perhaps I did it to myself. Who knows? My trust in God's love continually carries me through the ongoing ordeal. God's presence is always with me. God's love is expressed to me concretely through caring family and friends who stand by me, pray with me, and take care of me in my times of need. I am not used to being the one cared for; it takes some adjusting. I have always been the one caring for others. It continues to be a wonderful growth experience, a learning process.

Parents need to nurture in their children a love of God that can serve as an anchor throughout life. Starting in the early childhood years, encourage a sense of wonder and awe at the miracles of God's creation. Learn to appreciate the beauty of nature and the miracle of our own bodies. Teach children to thank God often and audibly. While saying grace at meals, let it be a spontaneous prayer of thanks. As children get older, talk about Jesus' life and the lessons he taught. Keep religious pictures, books, magazines, and statues around the house. Someone once asked at a workshop, "If being Catholic was a criminal offense, punishable by death, could enough evidence be gathered from your home to convict you?" A thought to consider.

Perhaps I should caution parents about an inherent danger in prayers of petition. Sometimes we have a tendency to ask God for many things we think we need. As adults, we understand that often the answer to requests is NO, but young children have difficulty understanding this concept. If they are taught at too young an age that God hears and answers all our prayers, when their "wish" does not come true their trust in God is weakened. This can be spiritually devastating when dealing with illness. If Grandma dies, despite all the prayers, God becomes the "bad guy." Concentrate on teaching young children to ask God to be with the person who needs extra strength during a time of stress. Put the person (or pet) in God's care.

Discussion Questions

1. Think of someone whom you really trust. List the qualities that inspire trust.

2. Discuss a time someone you trusted let you down. Could you reestablish trust? What steps did you both take? How long did the rebuilding take?

3. When you were a teenager, what made you feel that your parents did/did not trust you? How did it make you feel?

Chapter 2

Individuality

Romans 15:7—
"Welcome one another, therefore, just as Christ has welcomed you, for the glory of God."

• Appreciating Unique Personalities

Although we have all learned that we are unique and unrepeatable images of God, how deeply do we believe it and truly appreciate our individuality? All persons have gifts, talents, and abilities specific to them. As parents, our task is to recognize the special qualities of each child and nurture his or her growth.

The truth of this fact hit home forcefully when my daughter was ten years old. After attending a workshop on self-esteem, I was reading *Please Understand Me.*[4] The book contains a short quiz based on the Myers-Briggs personality inventory. My daughter asked if she could take the test. As we scored the two tests, our basic personality differences became very apparent. Although there are many aspects to the personality inventory, each on a continuum from strong to mild, the introvert/extrovert area remains the most memorable to me. For years I had been pushing Kristina, a strong introvert, to be more social, more outgoing, a "party animal" like me, a strong extrovert.

Please Understand Me explains that extroverts are energized by being with people; introverts are drained by socializing. Extroverts love parties; going to a cocktail party terrorizes introverts. Extroverts talk to hear themselves talk; introverts are quiet, speaking only when they really have something to say. If nothing is going on, extroverts will make something happen; introverts are content to be "left to their own devices." Studies indicate that only about 25% of the American population are introverts. However, of those people considered "gifted," 60% are introverts.

After reading the book I learned better ways to handle my daughter, appreciating her immense talents in the fine arts areas of music, dance, art, and poetry. I stopped pushing her to go to parties, especially "sleepovers," which she hated. I try to allow her to be the person God designed her to be.

Doing research into the area of personality differences helps parents realize how unique each child is, how one sibling differs from the other, and most important, how children differ from their parents. Similarly, recognizing that children learn in different ways allows parents to nurture children's strengths and minimize focus on their weaknesses.

• Learning Styles Differ

Studies in multiple intelligences have shown eight major learning styles. Current educational systems are geared for the most part to linguistic and logical learners, neglecting the strengths of children who learn best by other means. Linguistic learners have excellent command of language, enjoy reading, writing, talking, arguing, debating. Logical learners manipulate concepts, preferring questioning, reasoning, problem solving, and mathematics. Children with these talents succeed well in a structured educational system.

Where does that leave children with strengths in the other six styles of learning? What about the musical learner who learns best through creating songs and rhythms? Physical learners need a hands-on approach to studying, being actively involved and moving around. Spatial learners have the ability to form mental images of things, are gifted with creative imaginations and artistic abilities. Naturalist learners concentrate on appreciating and exploring the world of nature, enjoying connections between nature and other subjects.

Lastly, *inter*personal learners flourish when allowed to learn in groups, sharing ideas and discussing information. This type of learning, however, does not work well with *intra*personal learners who tend to turn more inward, preferring to study in solitude, away from noise and confusion, being more self-reflective. This type of learner detests being forced into group projects.[5]

Although the above gives only the briefest sketch of lengthy research, *Eight Ways of Knowing* creatively points out to parents and teachers ways of helping children by playing up their strengths and strengthening their weaknesses. The many exercises described in the book enhance the variety of learning capabilities within every youngster, thus increasing success in classroom situations.

Never compare children to one another, whether siblings, relatives, or friends. Irreparable damage can occur. Everyone needs to be appreciated for the things he or she does well, not criticized for areas of weakness. Work with children to maximize their individual potential.

• Family Constellation—Always Unique

Respecting individual differences also encompasses allowing children a right to privacy. Establish some kind of space where each child can keep personal belongings that are of special value to him or her. Siblings must be taught to respect each other's space, not trespassing or taking things without asking. Not all possessions need to be shared. Let children put away items they prefer to protect from the possibility of being broken by other children. Think about how you feel when your belongings are taken without permission. Children feel the same way. The concept of sharing is difficult for all people to learn. The younger the child, the more difficult the lesson. Encourage sharing, but do not demand it!

Speaking of siblings, studies on family constellation indicate many differences exist among only children, oldest children, middle children, and youngest children. Often only children get a reputation for being spoiled, self-centered, and selfish. However, because they spend a lot of time alone, they also develop resourcefulness in amusing themselves. Oldest children are thought of as more responsible, desiring to please, help, and protect others. Youngest children are often assumed to be spoiled because they are "the baby." Some play up this position by becoming helpless, while others rebel against the label. Middle children seem to be concerned with justice and equality, with the middle child of a three children family having the most difficult time. Middle children in larger families learn to adapt and cooperate.[6]

Recently published, *The New Birth Order Book: Why You Are the Way You Are* contains extremely interesting insights into these issues. Controversy does surround the study of family constellations, since each family is influenced by many factors. This book explores the many variables that exist within families which affect any conclusions that are reached and the effects of variables on personality development. It makes for interesting speculation.

I remember mentioning to a friend when my boys were young that they were *so* different, not only in physical appearance, but also in personality. She asked if I had heard of the "Second Child Syndrome." I had to admit that I had not! She explained that the first child arrives on the scene and decides who he or she wants to be from an open field. When the second child appears, one slot is taken, so that child tries to be as totally different from the firstborn as possible. It may not be scientific, but it seems to work!

When Joseph was nearly six, Kristina entered our "family constellation," usurping his position as "baby" of the family. He was less than thrilled at being deposed. In fact, he will always bear the stigma of "middle child," even though since he was over five years of age when his sister was born it supposedly negates his middle child personality. I continually tell him to start a "Poor Me Club" for middle children. There are plenty of people eager to join and share their tales of being "neglected," including several of his cousins. Easy for me to say; I am an oldest!

Parents often comment about how differently their children all turned out, when they "raised them all the same." At an informative parenting workshop given by psychologist Richard Fowler, Ph.D., I learned that parents *cannot* parent each child in the same way. Dr. Fowler made parallel columns, describing how parents are constantly changing physically, emotionally, psychologically, financially, and spiritually. Children arrive at a specific point in a person's life, then the child starts to grow and mature. As another child arrives, the parents are in a different place from when the first child arrived. Dynamics change and life goes on.

I remember to this day one of Dr. Fowler's comments about the unfairness of life. Often as parents are entering their stage of "Midlife Transition" (38–45), their children are entering adolescence (12–17). This makes for some really interesting family dynamics as everyone learns new coping skills.[7]

A final comment regarding appreciation of each child's individuality involves parents having developmentally appropriate expectations. A good parenting handbook, such as a series published by the American Academy of Pediatrics (see Appendix 1), helps parents understand human growth and development. Reading in print what skills children typically have at what age reassures parents that behaviors are appropriate to a child's age. Enjoy them at each stage.

Stress is created when parents expect more from children than children are capable of performing. They are not miniature adults. Their attention span is about one minute per year of age! They must move around. The vocabulary of a three year old consists of about 700 words. They might not understand what you are saying. Directions need to be very specific and given one step at a time. Their memories are developing. How many times have you heard mothers yelling at children to act their age when in reality that is exactly what they are doing? Be patient; they mature.

Discussion Questions

1. Each family member is unique and special. List the most lovable qualities of each member of the family. How do these qualities enrich the family?

2. From the brief description given, where do you see yourself falling on an introvert/extrovert scale of one to ten? Where do other family members fall? How does this affect family relations?

3. People's interests vary. Thinking back to early school years, what school subjects most interested you? How was this interest nurtured?

Chapter 3

Mealtimes

Proverbs 17:1—
"Better a dry morsel with quiet than a house full of feasting with strife."

• Sacredness of Mealtime

In the rush-rush world of today, fast food becomes a staple of everyday life. A working mother told me that her young daughter doesn't ask, "What's for dinner?" when picked up from daycare. Rather, she asks, "Where are we picking up dinner?" The mother explained that she decided on this trade-off to cooking dinner because it gave her more time to sit down and enjoy her family.

No matter what the food is, or how it gets on the table, effort needs to be made in establishing family meals occasionally during the week. Sitting together peacefully, while carrying on civil conversations, teaches children communication skills that last a lifetime. Communication keeps family members connected to one another and builds family unity.

Mealtime is truly "sacred" time; turn off the television, do not answer the telephone, refrain from arguing, scolding, and lecturing. Family meetings can be held after the meal is eaten to discuss issues of concern. An aura of calm aids digestion. Table manners need to be taught gently, not creating an atmosphere of dread.

Make mealtime a special event by using candles, flowers, and table decorations, especially when the children help create them. Modeling this "specialness" of mealtime helps children learn the significance of participating in the eucharistic celebration. Explaining how we as a Catholic Christian community come together around the table of the Lord to break bread and give thanks at liturgy is more easily understood when children experience family meals.

Mealtimes are the perfect time to pray together. Practice "spontaneous prayer." Let everyone give thanks for something that happened that day, or pray for a special intention. Experience speaking to God from your heart; it is not hard once you get used to it! You can always fall back on "Bless us, O Lord...," but encourage creativity even when it comes out "Thank you God for mashed potatoes."

I used to be jealous of my Baptist aunt who created the most beautiful grace before meals when we ate at her house. She would bless the farmers who grew the food, the cooks who prepared the food, the family and friends joined around the table. It was very moving. At our house we prayed before every meal, but it was always the same prayer. Now, after years of practice, I can finally create my own special prayers. Most of my family prefers, however, to fall back on the familiar.

Years ago, friends gave us a beautiful family prayer, printed on a Valentine, that they used as an echo prayer. I love it. Our family learned it. We use it on special occasions. It makes everyone cry. I do not know the source.

God Our Father has made us a family.
As members of one another,
I need you and you need me.
I love you and you love me.
I forgive you and you forgive me.

24

We work together and we play together.
We listen to God's Word and make it our own together.
Together we reach out to others and share with them our oneness.
Together we hope to rise and enjoy eternal new life.
This is our faith, our hope, our way of life as a family.
May the Spirit within us draw us closer,
until we are one in the Lord.
Amen.

My husband usually leads while we echo each phrase. One evening our pastor came for dinner, so we decided to join hands and recite this prayer. The boys were probably around eight and ten years old. During the prayer, I glanced over to see them arm wrestling! Looking furtively at Father, I could see him chuckling to himself!

• Avoiding Mealtime Conflict

After talking to a group of parents about the importance of mealtime, a father shared that he was so tired of disciplining his young children about table manners every night that one night he declared a "pig night." He took away the utensils, making the children use their fingers. Of course, they loved it! Now they beg to have more pig nights. If they try hard for a week to exhibit good manners, the reward is a pig night. This may not be acceptable to all families, but it would certainly take the children by surprise. They also learn that using utensils makes eating food easier.

Food easily becomes the subject of power struggles between parents and children, quickly escalating to no-win situations. When neither party will give in to the other, disaster follows. In order to avoid such battles, there are a few simple guidelines to remember. Help on food issues can be found in the American

Academy of Pediatrics' book *Guide to Your Child's Nutrition* (see Appendix 1).

Young children have small stomachs that cannot hold the same amount of food as that of an adult. Eating small amounts six times a day is more appropriate. Make sure the food items they are getting are nutritious—fruits, vegetables, cheese, crackers, and meat items.

Children have food preferences, too. Let them help plan weekly menus so that they feel they are making choices. Try a variety of foods, including those parents might personally dislike. Expand your tastes. Fruits and vegetables are essential to a healthy diet. If unsure about preparation of certain items, ask a market produce manager. He or she is usually anxious to help. Parents might discover new foods to enjoy, also. Help children experience "food adventures."

Everyone goes through phases of food preferences; sometimes we call them cravings. Children are no different. One week they might love macaroni and cheese, then the next week refuse to touch it. Pediatric studies indicate that over the the period of one month, the children studied consumed the same amount of calories and balanced nutrition when offered a variety of healthy foods. Parents do not need to run a short-order kitchen. Offering a choice of two items should suffice. My mother often commented on the fact that I frequently served two vegetables at dinner. It was not for the children's sake, although they benefited from it. Their father refuses to eat certain vegetables that I happen to love.

When our daughter decided to become a vegetarian during her teen years, we compromised. She found recipes; I bought the ingredients. She cooked; we ate what she fixed. We all learned more about nutrition and expanded our tastes. When I was diagnosed with breast cancer, the oncologist said to avoid red meat, eat limited amounts of fish and chicken, eat fresh fruits and vegetables, and add soy protein to my diet. Kristina was on the right track all along.

A basic tenet of discipline states that behavior which is rewarded will repeat itself. Parents have difficulty realizing that children do not care if attention is positive or negative; it is still attention. When a parent spends an inordinate amount of time arguing over food with a child, that child has the parent trapped in interaction. *The time spent together is a reward.* How much better it is to spend the time together in a positive way. We used to tell our children there would be no dessert if they did not eat their dinner. Joseph consistently replied that he did not want dessert anyway! End of discussion. However, there are no bedtime snacks—next meal is breakfast.

• Heritage of Family Meals

As children get older and become more involved in after-school activities, families have to work harder to hold on to family mealtimes. When our boys were in high school, dinner sometimes occurred at eight o'clock. Healthy snacks were furnished to those awaiting the arrival of the last person. The important thing to us was spending time together.

Catching children at home for meals means being creative. Let them have friends come over. Let them do the cooking. Teach them how to barbecue. Let them show off to friends. Hold pizza and movie nights. Do whatever it takes!

Weekend brunch became family time, when sports did not interfere, allowing teens to sleep in until a reasonable hour. Liturgy focused on youth was Sunday evening, enabling us to have relaxed Sunday mornings. (And, do not stress out about how they look when they go to church; at least they are going with you.

It is sometimes a lesson in humility for parents. Anyone who criticizes has never raised a teenager.)

Often we would meet other families at church, then go out to eat together—usually "fast food." Going to church became more than attending liturgy; it truly became a sharing, faith-filled community experience. Now that our children have grown up, several couples from our church community still rendezvous each week and go out to eat. When circumstances occur and someone is missing, the experience of community is diminished. God calls us to be in relationship with one another, just as God wants to be in relationship with each of us.

Our adult children, away from home, yearned for that feeling of community. Attending a church where they knew nobody was not the same. When they were home from college, they looked forward to attending church as an opportunity to see friends. Now, as they form their own families, our young adults are searching for parishes where they can make friends and establish a similar sense of community.

Attending a conference entitled "Religious Orientations of Baby Boomers and Generation X: Implications for Ministry" made me see that this search for a sense of community is common to most young adults. Results of a national study were published in a book entitled *The Search for Common Ground* (see Appendix 1). The church is losing vast numbers of young adults to other denominations in which their needs for relationships are being met. As a faith community, we need to pay attention and find ways of promoting fellowship in Catholic parishes.

Extended families have gotten smaller, and family members are often far apart because of employment opportunities. Getting together every Sunday at Granny's for a chicken dinner is a tradition from the past for most people. Holding tight to the value of family meals, celebrating holidays and special occasions together, inviting others to become part of the extended family, all help to keep family spirit alive and well and promote family unity.

Discussion Questions

1. Develop some discussion starters to use at mealtime to improve family communication. For example: What is the best thing that happened to you today? Did you learn anything new today?

2. Create a mealtime prayer of your own. Write it down and share it with your family.

3. Plan a special family dinner for the weekend. Let all family members make menu suggestions. Give assignments for table decorations, food preparation, and cleanup.

Chapter 4

Enthusiasm

Proverbs 15:13—
A glad heart makes a cheerful countenance, but by sorrow of heart the spirit is broken."

• "En Theos"—In the Spirit of God

In his book *On Parenting,* James Dobson states:

Throughout the Scriptures, it is quite clear that the raising of children was viewed as a wonderful blessing from God—a welcome, joyful experience. And today, it remains one of the greatest privileges in living to bring a baby into the world...a vulnerable little human being who looks to us for all his needs. What a wonderful opportunity it is to teach these little ones to love God with all their hearts and to serve their fellowman throughout their lives. There is no higher calling than that![8]

So—attack the call to parenting with *enthusiasm!* The word itself contains a clue on achieving success in the endeavor. *En theos* means "in God." Make God part of the parenting team. Create time to develop a prayer life. Establish a prayer routine. Rely on God for inspiration in times of need. The Latin root of "inspiration" means "to breathe in." Breathing in the Spirit of God calms, relaxes, clears the mind, and frees us to receive God's word in our hearts. Take time to listen for God's promptings during the franticness of each day.

When my children were young, I did a lot of my praying while carpooling. There always seemed to be waiting periods. Playing religious music in the car is prayer-filled to me. [Students in the carpool did not appreciate my taste in music. I would let them turn on their favorite radio stations, then we would get heated discussions going over lyrics.] Keeping spiritual reading material under the seat of the car helped fill in those times when waiting at the orthodontist, music lessons, ballfields, dance, tennis, or gymnastic lessons.

The simple "Jesus Prayer" is one of my favorite prayers. This prayer consists of simply breathing in deeply, holding the breath momentarily, then exhaling slowly. While you do this, close your eyes (unless you are driving) and meditate on "Je-" while breathing in and "-sus" while exhaling. It serves as a mantra, leading into a meditative state. Just relax and listen. God speaks in a very quiet voice.

During times of relaxed meditation, answers to problems often become apparent. Ideas that had not occurred to you before suddenly spring into your mind. A memory might be resurrected. People in your life might come to mind, calling you to contact them or pray for them. God has interesting ways of breaking into our lives. A wall plaque in my office says, "Coincidence is when God acts and chooses to remain anonymous."

• Watching for Miracles

Little miracles occur around us every day. Often we are too distracted to notice. M. Scott Peck explores this topic in *The Road Less Traveled*:

In thinking about miracles, I believe that our frame of reference has been too dramatic. We have been looking for the burning bush, the parting of the sea, the bellowing voice from heaven. Instead we should be looking at the ordinary day-to-day events in our lives for evidence of the miraculous, maintaining at the same time a scientific orientation.[9]

From there Peck goes on with many examples.

Slow down and appreciate the beauty and miracles of nature unfolding every day. Help children develop a sense of wonder and awe at what they notice. Pay attention to small details, calling children to examine things closely. Ever marvel at how a snail moves while carrying his house on his back? Have you watched a beautiful sunset develop and thanked God for the privilege? Have you looked for signs of the changing seasons, realizing that through the cycles of nature we come to trust that God is keeping the earth in existence? Learn to appreciate such miracles.

When I started teaching preschool catechesis in 1980, I had been a Catholic all my life. I had attended Catholic schools through college and graduate school. My faith and trust in God blossomed when I got down to a young child's level and started really looking at the world. Learning to verbalize my gratitude to the loving God who creates such marvels started becoming more natural. Soon my friends suggested that I had been "born again" because I would, without embarrassment, thank God out loud for a gorgeous sunset, or the colors of flowers, or the beauty of rain, or the warming rays of sunshine.

I learned to watch for Peck's "little miracles," and would share such occurrences with my friends and family. It really is amazing. One time a friend was putting her four year old on a flight back East to visit an aunt. The mother was terribly worried and had been praying about the situation. She "happened" to mention it to me. I "happened" to mention it to another friend.

Can you believe it? The second friend's young adult daughter was booked on the same flight. Coincidence? I don't think so!

• Taking Care of #1

To enhance enthusiasm for life, parents need to take good care of themselves physically, mentally, emotionally, and spiritually. Being a parent takes an enormous amount of energy. Proper rest, good nutrition, and exercise are all necessary components of good health. Maximize your energy level. Take care of yourself.

In order to take care of others, parents must learn to care of themselves. It is not selfishness to need private time and space to recharge your batteries. You can't give to others what you yourself haven't got. When drained, patience is short, nerves are on edge, problems seem worse.

Parents need to let the family know when they need a time-out. Lie down for fifteen minutes, walk around the block, soak in a hot bath (without the children banging on the door asking a million questions that just cannot wait—I've been there). Family members will soon appreciate the refreshed YOU that emerges. Eventually they may even suggest that you take a time-out when they sense you need it.

A spiritual director once asked me to list the things I did for myself. The question had me stumped. All I could come up with was getting my acrylic nails done every three weeks! Boy, did I get a lecture. Going to lunch with a friend, sitting and reading a novel for an hour, spending two hours wandering a mall by myself, walking at the beach. Could these actually be spiritual activities? What a unique concept. He "ordered" me to do one of these activities every day for a week and see how I felt. I did not believe that I deserved such leisure. At first, it was difficult to make time for myself. My husband might tell you that I have now taken those suggestions to new heights (but the children are grown and out of the house).

Lon calls my time with friends my "Coffee Shop Ministry." One day, while having breakfast with him at a coffee shop, we saw a woman wearing a "Roman collar" come in and meet with a group. She was evidently an Episcopalian priest. Lon said all I need is a collar. It has become a standing joke: "I'm off to do ministry!" One day, before I left friends whom I had met for breakfast, another friend arrived that I was meeting for lunch. Some days ministry can really be tough!

Start and end each day with prayer. I love wall plaques. I have them everywhere as reminders. One says, "Days hemmed in prayer are less likely to unravel." Ask God for help and guidance as you start a new day; tuck in areas where you feel you need special strength. Call on Mary and Joseph for their support. Remember, they were parents too. Sometimes they are portrayed as so holy that we forget they walked the floor with a teething Jesus, changed diapers, disciplined, worried over the rebellious adolescent who got lost. Enlist them as part of your parenting team.

As the day ends, thank God for the blessings received, the miracles that happened. As you drift off to sleep, do an "examination of conscience," *not* recounting failings but rather *affirming* all the good that you accomplished. Psychologists say that a person's last thoughts before sleep repeat in the mind throughout the night. Make those last thoughts positive and awaken with more enthusiasm for the challenges of the coming day.

Finally, develop a positive attitude toward parenting. Look for the joys and rewards. Share with friends what you enjoy most about being a parent. All parents know the sacrifices, work, and drudgery that accompany parenting. Too often those aspects are the main topics of discussion. Children hear what adults are saying. Negative attitudes can cause children to feel more of a burden than a blessing. Self-esteem improves when children hear how important they are to their parents and what happiness they provide. Think positive! Talk positive! Be enthusiastic!

Discussion Questions

1. List three possible things you could do to revitalize yourself. Where can you fit these into your schedule over the coming week?

2. Think about the last time you felt totally drained, unable to go on, exhausted. What symptoms told you to take a break? What did you do to alleviate the stress? Did it work? What better ways could you have handled the situation?

3. Discuss your attitude toward the importance of exercise. Where can it fit into your weekly schedule?

Section 2

Making TIME to Appreciate Family History

Chapter 5

Traditions

Proverbs 1:8—
"Hear, my child, your father's instruction, and do not reject your mother's teaching."

• Appreciating "Roots"

Children are born into a particular social setting. Sometimes roots are shunned when they should be nourished. Understanding who we are necessitates looking at where our ancestors originated. Science is continually proving the importance of genetics. Make time to look at the family tree. Research the history of ancestors that made the journey to America. Get older relatives to write down, or audio tape, memories of the stories they have been told. Much oral history is lost when families pay scant attention to the memory bank of the elderly. Go through family pictures and identify who the people in the photographs are before no one remembers the names.

My father's family history was lost because his older sister, who was his only sibling, died before writing down what she knew of their family tree. Having learned this lesson, we tried to get my father-in-law to record his memories of growing up in Minnesota, how he met my mother-in-law, what he knew of her family (she died many years ago), and any family history about his parents' emigration from Poland. We gave him a tape recorder and tapes for Christmas several years ago. He never got around to using it until one weekend when we stayed with him.

Working on scrapbooks for my children became my hobby, and I asked my father-in-law if he had any pictures of relatives. He pulled out boxes of pictures and we began looking through them. He started reminiscing. My husband got the recorder out and we captured a lot of family history. My father-in-law said sitting and talking into a recorder by yourself is hard, but having someone ask you questions, and the talking together, made the endeavor fun. He later died of cancer, so those tapes are treasured.

Develop an appreciation of cultural traditions from your family of origin. Are there rituals and celebrations that have been forgotten? Make it a family project to research the culture of the country from which the family came. What ethnic foods are part of the culture? Listen to music from the country of origin. Find out about dances, games, costumes. Celebrate the fact that you come from a family that added color and texture to the fabric of American life.

When two parents come from culturally diverse backgrounds, it is especially important for them to share and discuss customs, traditions, and values.

• Creating New Traditions

Each family develops its own style of living and within that style, traditions develop. Make time to insure that children appreciate those traditions which they can count on year after year. Children love traditions. Sometimes, after doing an activity twice, children see it as a tradition and come to expect repetitions. Many family traditions develop around holidays, especially Christmas.

Traditions

When I was growing up, my family opened presents from relatives on Christmas Eve, then "Santa gifts" arrived Christmas morning. My husband grew up with the tradition that nothing was opened until the family had attended Christmas morning Mass, eaten breakfast, and cleaned up the dishes. Then they sat in a circle while each child, of four siblings, took a turn opening one present at a time. This took quite a while. Children like to know the routine. It helps them cope with the excitement of holidays when they can predict in what order things will happen. We blended a little of both families' traditions into our own family traditions.

When our first child was born, Lon was a senior in medical school and very busy. I took my one-month-old baby to a "cut your own" tree lot, picked a tree, had it cut and stuffed into our Volkswagen Bug. For the next twenty-five Christmas seasons we returned to that lot, almost without fail. Thanksgiving weekend you would tag your tree and return to cut it, closer to Christmas. What a treasured family tradition, until recently, when the Christmas tree farm became a parking lot! Time for a new tradition—to our children's horror—an artificial tree!

Easter Egg hunts became a tradition for not only my children, but the nieces and nephews as well. Lon and I put notes in plastic eggs. Some notes say an amount of money, some say prize, some say candy, balloon, stickers, and the like. Each child at the Easter celebration gets to find one dozen eggs. They can not open their eggs until each one has found his or her share. This encourages older children to help younger ones. Then they collect their treats. Even the teenagers still want to participate in what has become known as "Aunt Marilyn's Dash for Cash."

Camping has been a "traditional" family vacation for many years. Relatives and other families join us in these adventures. Our children often bring friends along who have never had the opportunity to camp. We always have a good time. Without television and telephones, people are forced to talk together, play games, sing songs, and tell stories. (We discourage use of cellular phones, boom boxes, and computer games.) Enjoying God's gifts of nature while learning to relax and slow down are important life lessons. Activities like hiking, fishing, horseback riding, swimming, playing ball, or reading quickly fill the days.

Stargazing started as a camping activity, but has become another family tradition. Lon keeps track of the occurrence of meteor showers. We try to find a dark location to watch the sky. The children have learned to identify constellations and planets. We invested in a telescope with which we can see the rings of Saturn and the moons of Jupiter. Examining the universe puts in perspective the relationship of mankind to the order of God's world, of which we are a very small part.

• Religious Traditions Essential

Appreciation of God's place in our lives must develop throughout life. Religious traditions encourage children in their awareness of God's love for them. Simple traditions should begin from birth. Blessing a child with a short prayer and signing a cross on the forehead lets the child know that the parent believes in God's power to watch over and protect.

Saying grace before eating expresses gratefulness to God for the gifts of food, shelter, and family. Encouraging children to say prayers spontaneously, from their heart, teaches them that praying is simply talking to God, a habit that should continue throughout life.

The tradition of praying at bedtime with the children affords the opportunity to thank God for all the good things that happened, and to ask God's help to handle difficulties. This time can be an opening to wonderful discussions about their day.

Attending church services connects family traditions with the broader traditions of our faith family. Sunday Mass was not negotiable. When they were young, the children were easily bribed with the promise of a doughnut after Mass. As they entered the rebellious teen years, when they found Mass "boring," we rewarded them with breakfast or dinner out (even if it was fast food). Several families would meet at Mass, so the children could sit with their friends, then we would go eat together.

Christmas Midnight Mass became a favorite family tradition as the children got older, even though it meant "Santa" stayed up really late. Participating in activities to help the less fortunate remains an important family tradition, especially at Christmas. Lighting the candles on an Advent wreath each night at dinner helps mark the passage of time as we await the celebration of Christ's birth. Our children loved to take turns lighting and extinguishing the candles.

During Lent, our family traditions center more on "doing extra" rather than "giving up" things. Going to morning Mass as frequently as possible, saying a rosary, making a visit to church, and helping others by doing good deeds are popular activities. Turning off the television one night a week and playing board games was supposed to be a sacrifice, but most often turned out to be more fun than watching television.

Attending the Holy Thursday celebration, Good Friday's solemn services, and culminating with the Easter Vigil on Saturday night always helped to keep the family focused on the reason for Easter. The children loved the dark church on Saturday night when the "light of Christ" is passed. Watching them holding burning candles always caused concern, but they treasure those memories (and they never burned up the church or themselves).

The Catholic Church has an abundance of religious traditions from which a family can select. Devotions to particular saints, novenas, and holy days all provide opportunities to establish your own family religious traditions. Celebrating each family member's "saint day" by studying about the saint's life adds to the family's appreciation of its religious heritage. Traditions link the past with the present, and will carry our families into the future.

Discussion Questions

1. Thinking back to your childhood, share your most vivid Christmas morning memory.

2. Ask your children what the best vacation was that you have shared. Ask them why.

3. Tracing your roots, name the countries and cultures of your ancestors. If you do not know—start asking questions. WRITE IT DOWN!

Chapter 6

Inheritance

Proverbs 19:14—
"House and wealth are inherited from parents, / but a prudent wife is from the LORD."

• How YOU Were Parented

Once again we turn our attention to the family in which you were raised. As a couple comes together to establish a new family unit, the partners should be encouraged to look at their family of origin to see how they were influenced during their maturing years. Ethnic and cultural considerations have been previously discussed. Now we look more specifically at how each person was parented. This becomes key in understanding psychological makeup and behavior.

Every family has strengths and weaknesses. Being able to examine objectively the family in which you grew up, recognizing both the good and bad aspects, is essential. You can then formulate a plan for raising your children. Professional help is needed to overcome extreme problems, such as having a mentally ill, alcohol- or drug-abusing parent, or a physically or emotionally abusive, or distant parent.

Families differ, parenting styles differ, and times change. Discipline techniques used by parents during childhood are extremely influential. Whether you were raised in an authoritarian environment (given little freedom of choice or power in decision making) or, at the other extreme, in a permissive home (where a lack of structure, no firm rules, and constantly changing schedules resulted in disorder), you *are* the product of your early childhood years.

When parents come from homes where discipline techniques varied greatly, conflict over how their children will be raised is inevitable. Rational thought and planning must go on *before* issues arise so that parents present a unified front on any particular issue. If a child sees a crack in the parental front, he or she will wedge right in and widen the gap. Soon the parents are fighting, the child disappears, and the issue remains unsettled!

Even with the best of intentions, when stress occurs, psychologists tell us that we revert to parenting the way we were parented. If you did not like the way you were parented, then try to be more diligent than others in overcoming a repetition of mistakes. Communication with each other is essential. When giving parenting workshops, one of the most frequently mentioned problems is the lack of agreement between parents on matters of discipline. This causes stress within the marriage. Children are very quick to figure out how to utilize this discord to their advantage.

Education in parenting skills is very helpful. My son, after witnessing some very poor parenting occurring at his neighbors' home, said he thought parents should be required to pass a test before leaving the hospital with a baby. "After all, you need a license to drive a car!" Children, unfortunately, do not come with "how-to" manuals. Parents must learn as they go, often without the benefit of extended family modeling and support.

A clipping I saved says it all: "You won't learn much from the mistakes you made with your first child, because every child is completely different. You'll make a completely new set of mistakes with each one."

When my youngest child started junior high, I returned to school to study for a master's degree. My wisdom increased; however, the knowledge came too late for many issues. I remember coming home and announcing at dinner one evening that in studying psychologist Rudolf Dreikurs' theories, I learned that you should never do anything for children that children can do for themselves. Therefore, I was instituting a new family policy of everybody taking responsibility for themselves. My children asked their father to make me quit school! He denied their request. (My daughter constantly tells me that "Dad is sooooo spoiled!" Training him has failed!)

Systematic Training for Effective Parenting (see Appendix 1) remains my favorite program for teaching parents practical and easy-to-understand techniques for dealing with parent/child issues. Workshops provide parents with opportunities to share concerns and explore more effective techniques for gaining cooperation within the family. The time spent in a workshop series is well worth the effort, but even studying the workbook on your own can provide amazing help. Many parents have sent thank-you notes for my recommendation of this program.

• Genetics Plays Important Role

Basic temperament is something with which we are born. Newborns show signs at birth of being easygoing or high-strung. Many facets of personality come through our genetic structure. Family traits in personality can be seen as easily as physical traits. Understanding ourselves helps us deal better with family members. Taking personality inventories, such as the one included in *Please Understand Me* (see Appendix 1), the Myers-Briggs, or the

Enneagram, provides clues to a deeper understanding of how we function in relation to others.

Genetics plays an important role in health also. Scientists continually discover new information about genetically linked diseases. Awareness of health problems which might be inherited enables a person to take preventive measures. My family has a very poor heart history. My father died of a heart attack at thirty-eight years of age, my brother at forty-six. I know the risks and try to live a healthy lifestyle. My mother-in-law died of colon cancer at fifty-six years *young*. My husband knows the risks and has periodic colon screening tests. With today's improved medical knowledge, procedures, and treatments, we are able to deal with genetic issues more successfully.

Addictive personalities have a genetic component that families need to acknowledge and discuss. For too long person suffering from alcoholism was a skeleton in the family closet. Children need to be warned early if there is a family weakness in handling alcohol or drugs. Vigilant watch must be kept for symptoms requiring treatment. Help should be sought, rather than the issue avoided.

Obesity sometimes runs in families because of addiction to food, but obesity in general is becoming an epidemic problem in America, especially among children and teenagers. Health risks are extreme for obese people, so steps must be taken to keep families healthy and active. Many studies show direct correlation between obesity in children and the amount of television watched. Physical inactivity and the assault of commercials for fattening foods is a disastrous combination.

Spend time researching family trees for medical histories, ask relatives, find out about traits and recurring illnesses. Encourage older relatives to be truthful in relating such information as it could have direct bearing on YOUR future. Write down your findings so the knowledge may be passed on to future generations.

• Economic Expectations

The word *inheritance* brings to mind trust funds and "lifestyles of the rich and famous." Every person is raised in an economic climate that affects attitudes and expectations. When two people unite in forming a family unit, it is imperative that they discuss their expectations for the future. Finances play a tremendous role in marital strife, no matter what the economic bracket.

Those raised in lower income situations may have life somewhat easier in the long run because their expectations are lower. My father died young, leaving my mother with three children, aged nine, seven, and two. She typed envelopes at home on a manual typewriter to earn money to feed, clothe, and house us until my youngest brother started elementary school. Someone once said to me that we must have been very poor when I was growing up, but I never knew it. I give my mother the credit for our never feeling that we were poor. We always had clothes (from Penney's or Sears), healthy food (mostly home cooked—eating out was a treat), and our own home. My parents bought a house six months before my father's death. My mother eventually paid off the mortgage and lived there until she died. She sent all three of us through Catholic elementary and high schools. I studied hard and received a California State scholarship that enabled me to go to college and get a good job.

My husband's father was a master carpenter who worked in construction while his wife stayed home raising four children. They lived a modest lifestyle, remaining in the house they purchased in 1943 until 1965. There were not a lot of luxuries. Vacations usually meant a drive to Minnesota to visit relatives. Medical bills for my mother-in-law depleted their finances. My husband received a California State scholarship that enabled him to attend college. With diligent study, he went on to enter and complete medical school.

Being college sweethearts, we wanted to eventually marry. I got a job with IBM paying enough that we decided to get married after the first year of medical school. Money was tight, but we were used to that. Our friends were all in the same boat. We were always clipping coupons to save money. Big splurges for Lon and me were burgers and a movie, when his medical school schedule allowed.

My personal belief is that those raised in affluence come to expect affluence. I have noticed with our own children that they take much of what they have received for granted. There was little financial struggle in their early lives. We wanted their lives to be easier than ours had been. Now that they are married, the boys are realizing how much their parents have done for them. It might have been easier on them now if we had taught fiscal responsibility earlier in life. Take heed.

Teaching children money management skills should start in the preschool years. Giving a small weekly allowance as part of sharing family resources should not be tied directly to household responsibilities, according to many parent educators. The two need to be independent, so that children do family duties because they are part of the family. Everyone helps. If jobs are done by children for monetary reward, when they do not need money, they do not feel they need to do any of the work.

A wonderful resource book for helping parents figure out how to teach financial planning skills is *Money Doesn't Grow on Trees*. The authors have a different slant on tying allowance to chores than some psychologists do, but their background is finance. They feel parents work hard for their money and should reasonably expect the children to put out some effort to earn their allowance. Work for pay teaches responsibility.[10] Parents should evaluate which philosophy works best in their situation.

As children get older, the amount of allowance should increase to cover school lunches, entertainment, clothing purchases, savings, and charitable contributions, especially church. Children learn to budget their money in early years through the natural consequence of squandering the money immediately, then waiting a week for their next allowance. This eliminates a lot of in-store disputes about wanting things. They either have the money, or it has already been spent. Detailed plans for teaching children the value of money are contained in *A Penny Saved*.[11]

Readily admitting that financial responsibility was our weakest area of parenting, we did always try to make our children realize the over-inflation of "designer labels." One incident that remains with me occurred at an after-Christmas outing to the mall when our son was about fourteen. He needed a new pair of tennis shoes, part of basic clothing for which we paid. Handing over sixty dollars, his father told him that if he wanted more expensive shoes he would have to come up with the difference from his Christmas money. He and his friend went off. When we rendezvoused at the designated time, Joe proudly showed us the shoes he found for $29.95, and the shirt he purchased with the balance. If we had been shopping with him, he would have tried to get us to buy him $100.00 shoes. When it is *their* money they are spending, children learn to look for bargains.

Discussion Questions

1. Rate your family of origin on a scale of one to ten—with one being totally permissive and ten being totally authoritarian. Rate your spouse's family. How do these methods of parenting affect you currently?

2. How complete is your medical history? Make up a "causes of death" family tree for your personal information and that of your children.

3. Do both spouses hold the same perspective on spending/saving and planning for the future? Discuss your children's attitude toward the value of money.

Chapter 7

Memories

Proverbs 10:7—
"The memory of the righteous is a blessing."

• What Is Remembered?

Sometimes we have to slow down and reflect on what we are doing with our time. When one day flows into another we lose track of time. Perhaps our pace of living is too fast. Many people talk about memory loss, looking for medical help, or herbal cures. This might just be a sign of stress, a warning to savor the time God gives us, especially family time.

Talk with your children about things that they remember. Get them in the habit of reflecting on past events. Find out what activities they most enjoy, which vacations held special meaning. Take your clues from their responses. Let them help plan family outings.

Do not get discouraged by children's favorite memories. One summer after taking a driving/camping vacation that encompassed Mt. Rushmore, the Grand Canyon, Carlsbad Caverns, and many natural wonders in between, my father-in-law asked the children what they thought was the most impressive sight. Their reply was the rooftop swimming pool at the hotel where we splurged on our final night of travel!

Building a Family

Working together to plan a family vacation can be an all-year project. Send away for information about where you will be going. The Chambers of Commerce are always happy to help. Discuss what you want to see and do, how finances will be budgeted. Let children assist in setting goals. Helping to save money for the long-awaited vacation teaches financial planning. Excitement escalates when all are contributing. Memories are made!

Giving each family member an assignment for the vacation keeps everyone involved (depending on the ages of the children). One person can be navigator (reading and following maps), another the secretary (keeping a scrapbook), the treasurer can watch the budget, and the historian is in charge of the camera! Everyone has a hand in making the family vacation a truly memorable event.

Birthdays are important to children, or really to all of us. Children look forward all year to that big day. Do not disappoint them, but likewise do not overwhelm them. Birthday parties should be memorable for the good times. All too often the "birthday child" ends the event in tears. Parents feel like failures. The day becomes a disaster. (Parents often attempt to cram too much quality time into too little of quantity time.) Let the child participate in planning the celebration. Make activities age appropriate. Do not let the size of the gathering overwhelm the birthday child. A rule of thumb is one guest per year of age. Introverts, like my daughter, are happier with even smaller groups. She liked to take one friend to an amusement park!

Keep parties reasonable. Exuberant parents of two year olds may hire clowns for their children's parties. Two year olds most often are terrified of clowns. Be aware. Magicians can have a very difficult time holding the attention of a group of preschoolers. Young children's attention spans are naturally short. They need physical activities. Do not expect more than they are capable of at their age.

Simplicity should be the key. What do children of a particular age enjoy doing? How long will the party continue? How much time can you reasonably expect the children to behave? Do you have a planned timetable to keep things moving? Have you thought about control and discipline? Will there be a sufficient number of adults present? Do not set yourself up for failure. Take pictures. Make happy memories.

• Creating Memories

In the hectic pace of life, few events really stand out as special. As we rush from activity to activity, sometimes we cannot recall what we did last week. I often wonder—if required to testify about my whereabouts at a given time, could I even remember?

Occasionally we need to make something memorable happen. Surprise your spouse. Surprise your children. Surprise yourself. Take a risk. Do the unexpected. Go on a picnic. Visit a museum. Lounge around in pajamas and play games. Do whatever it takes to reconnect as a family, so you remember what being a family is all about. The children will treasure "the day we all played hooky!"

With three children, it was sometimes difficult to make sure each one received individual attention. We instituted "special dates," when one parent and one child did something special together. It might be a bike ride, a movie, flying a kite, going to a park or the beach, or eating a meal out. My favorite memory is an evening my son says he does not even recall, but the important thing is, I do!

When asked what he wanted to do for our "special date," he replied that he wanted to take me out to dinner, but "not to some sleazy joint" (his words). He wanted me to wear a dress and high heels. He was even willing to wear the First Communion suit he had recently acquired. What a fun night! He told me it was "okay to have a glass of wine." He knew Dad would have bought me a glass of wine. We held hands across the table as we talked, waiting for our food to arrive. He was a perfect little gentleman. Memories like that make parenting very worth while!

Joining community programs designed to encourage family time help build bonds and memories. Lon remains grateful that someone introduced him to the YMCA Indian Guide/Princess program. This well-organized program promotes time together for father and child. Lon and Kevin joined in 1975, developing friendships that are still strong today. Activities such as camping, fishing, hiking, snorkeling, kayaking, to name a few, provide tremendous bonding experiences. Joey joined them when he entered kindergarten. Lots of pictures chronicle their adventures.

Lon used to come home from outings making fun of the fathers of girls. He would joke about the girls having their fathers wrapped around their little fingers! Surprise! Surprise! In 1977 Kristina was born, so in 1982 he became an Indian Princess father, coping with braids, ponytails, and tantrums. Growth experiences were had by all. They have an especially close bond to this day, which I attribute to the time they spent together when she was young.

Make time to spend with your children during the early, formative years. The bonds will last a lifetime. Good communication skills developed during those years will help get parents through the turbulent years of adolescence.

• Keeping Memories Alive

If we forget to make time to reminisce over the wonderful times we have shared as family, memories remain dormant.

Strengthening family ties by spending time looking back over the years reminds us of the importance of family.

The main reason people take photos, slides, movies, and videos is to record for posterity the events that take place. How often these valuable memories are put away in boxes and closets! All but forgotten, they remain untouched. Make time to get these items out, look them over, tell the stories—over and over again. Children love to hear stories about themselves and see how they changed through the years.

A family tradition we enjoyed was getting the slides and 8mm movies out each year at the child's birthday, letting him or her pick the years to view. Lots of good-natured teasing went on over the funny clothes we wore, the weird hairstyles, and especially my husband's sideburns, long curly hair, and black-rimmed glasses. Hey, we were products of the seventies!

When our middle son was planning his wedding, his fiancée asked me to get pictures together for creation of a video to be shown at the rehearsal dinner. That project involved going through hundreds of 35mm slides, spanning many years. I decided it was the opportunity to sort special pictures out for each child. I created my own makeshift video for each child by video-taping the projected slides. We showed our daughter's video at her high school graduation party. What a hit!

My current project is creating a scrapbook for each child. Their "baby books" were woefully neglected, so I had to go back to 1969 to begin. Getting prints from slides becomes expensive. I have learned to be selective. Viewing the pictures year by year brings back a flood of forgotten memories. Writing the stories that go with the pictures insures that the stories will not be lost.

Luckily for me, my daughter-in-law represents a company that deals in scrapbook paraphernalia, so she keeps me organized and focused. Once a person gets going on such a project, realization of the importance of telling our stories occurs. The small details that a person remembers when photos trigger memories are truly amazing.

One picture from 1972 shows Kevin, at age three, sucking his thumb while rubbing Joey's head with his other hand. When Kevin's "blankey" was unavailable, he used his baby brother's head as a substitute. I had forgotten that frequent occurrence until I saw the picture. Now the story is recorded in both their scrapbooks.

As was discussed in the section on knowing about your family of origin, our family stories need to be recorded and handed down. I have heard that the reason older people reminisce about their lives is that it verifies and gives meaning to their existence. So be patient with us older people when we enjoy talking about our lives, experiences and memories. Throughout history oral tradition has been important. If extended families no longer gather to tell the stories, we must rely on the written word. I tell young families not to get thirty years behind as I did. Catching up is too hard!

Discussion Questions

1. Ask each family member to share a memory of his/her favorite vacation.

2. Have each child tell how he/she would like to celebrate next year's birthday. Start working on a plan.

3. As a family project, sort through pictures, talking about events. Start a scrapbook. If possible, let each child make his/her own scrapbook.

Chapter 8

Enjoyment

Proverbs 15:30—
"The light of the eyes rejoices the heart and refreshes the body."

• TIME—Children's Best Reward

Children need to feel important to their parents. Gaining that sense of worth comes from the time parents spend with their children. One of the most difficult discipline concepts for parents to accept stems from the axiom "Behavior which is rewarded will repeat itself." *Time is the reward,* and children do not care whether they gain the time for positive or negative behavior.

If a child can engage a parent, one on one, over a matter of misbehavior, the child still has been rewarded with the parent's time. Then the misbehavior will likely be repeated. How much better family life could be if parents spent time acknowledging, thus rewarding, the good behaviors with their time and attention. Consequently, good behaviors would be repeated more frequently.

Caught up in busy schedules, parents often overlook the helpful accomplishments of children. When the child becomes *uncooperative,* the behavior jumps right out and grabs the parent's attention. Then lecturing, reasoning, and arguing ensue.

Building a Family

Make a dedicated effort for one week to emphasize the positive. "Catch them being good." Ignore the minor, negative annoyances. Watch the atmosphere of the home improve. Enjoy your family more. Stress out less. Simple time-out procedures remove the reward of parents' time, give children a chance to regain control of themselves, and allow a cool-down period.

One friend told me that sending her children to their rooms was not effective, since they had too many "things" in the room with which to play. She required the misbehaving child to sit on the floor of the bathroom for the designated time. There were very few distractions there! She has five children, so I figure she had more experience in this area than I had.

Spend more time rewarding children by making time to go to a park, read a story, play catch, teach a card game (like *Fish* or *War*), play board games or work puzzles. A helpful book entitled *Let's Make a Memory* (see Appendix 1) has many wonderful activities for families.

Following my breast cancer surgery, I was forced to slow down for a few weeks. Remembering a suggestion from that book, I asked my husband to pick up a 1500-piece jigsaw puzzle. The book promised lots of family fun. The promise was fulfilled. We cleared the "formal" dining room table, which was seldom used, and commenced. That puzzle was like a people magnet. Family and friends gathered around to help. Many hours of conversation and laughter were shared. Everyone enjoyed it so much that we bought and worked several puzzles; then we coated them with puzzle glue, framed them, and hung them in my husband's pediatric examination rooms. Patients enjoy our efforts, and we enjoyed our family project.

• Keep a Sense of Humor

Look for the humorous side of situations when parenting. Be silly once in a while. Do the unexpected. Laugh a lot. Keep a loaded camera handy to record silly events. When my boys were young, looking at the humorous side of things saved me from losing my cool many times. My motto is: You can either laugh or cry; I choose to laugh!

Kevin used to love emptying his dresser drawers when he was two years old. There he would be, sitting in the middle of the room on a pile of clothes, or sitting in an empty drawer that he had pulled free. I have photographic proof to show him today as he deals with his two year old.

When Joey got old enough to be a playmate, the kids would really get into some situations that could try a mother's sense of humor, especially when they were outdoors. If things got too quiet, I always became suspicious. One favorite activity was digging a large hole, filling it with water, removing their shoes and socks, rolling up their pants legs, and stomping around making "gushy mud." What good was yelling? I had a hose, a washing machine, and a bathtub.

My husband found it quite humorous, on the occasions when he was called upon to make the children's school lunches, to leave the plastic wrap on cheese slices. When they bit into their sandwiches, they knew Dad had made the lunches. They learned to check before biting.

Helping children develop a sense of humor is another facet of parenting. The ability to laugh at one's foibles and mistakes makes the journey through life easier. God gifts human beings with a sense of humor, an essential component of being human. Animals cannot laugh at themselves. However, this gift often gets stifled early in life. Once suppressed, reviving it in adulthood becomes difficult. Infants have an inborn desire to smile. Those smiles are rewarded with much attention. The laughter of children must certainly be God's favorite kind of praise.

A favorite picture in my office is one of a "laughing Jesus." To be so well loved by his many followers, Jesus must have had a terrific sense of humor. Reread the gospels looking for the humor. It is there. Think of Zacchaeus in the tree—certainly that made Jesus smile.

God must get many laughs watching human beings deal with life. Maybe we should lighten up, not take ourselves too seriously. Cultivate the spirit of "let go—let God." Ninety percent of what we worry about never happens. Most of what does happen to us in life is out of our control, so why worry about all the possibilities?

Be spontaneous. Have fun. When you are at the park with children, don't just stand there, go down a slide, take a turn on the swing. Let out the child within you. God is by your side enjoying the experience with you. God calls us to not merely survive the life with which we are gifted, but to thrive and enjoy our life. Give thanks!

• Laughing <u>with</u>, not <u>at</u>

In attempting to help children develop a sense of humor, caution must be exercised in the area of teasing. Taken to the extreme, teasing can become ridicule. Ridicule is a form of emotional abuse. Care must be taken to preserve children's self-esteem. Their emotions are fragile and can be easily crushed. Is that not true of all people, no matter what their age?

When the family is laughing about something, be sure to check that everyone sees the humor in the situation. It is essential to be laughing *with* one another and not *at* a particular family member. Siblings should not be allowed to harangue each other to the point of tears over issues that are emotionally painful. Physical problems, such as a prominent nose, large ears, or protruding teeth, should never become a family joke. Such damaging activity must never be tolerated in the home.

Children are people, too. Their feelings and emotions count. Too much of the humor in the media today is sarcasm and put-down. The word sarcasm is rooted in Greek, meaning "to tear the flesh." Humor at another person's expense is not really funny. If you are watching a program that perpetuates this form of humor, point out to children that this behavior is offensive. Even better, write to the station and the program sponsors. Children, like sponges, absorb media values. Parents are the filter needed to remove harmful influences.

Good-natured teasing seems to be part of family life. With three children, and a fun-loving husband, things have always been lively around our house. Surely there have been times when things have gotten somewhat out of hand. Intentions are never to degrade. Family members must know that they have the right to speak up if teasing becomes hurtful. Communication can solve problems; silence lets hurts fester.

Discussion Questions

1. What is the most common misbehavior of each child? How might your handling of the situation perpetuate the problem?

2. Describe a time when one of the children did something outrageous. Were you able to laugh, or did you lose your cool?

3. Thinking back to your childhood, tell about the most painful teasing you experienced. Who was the person teasing you? Have you forgiven the person?

Section 3

Making TIME for Communication

Chapter 9

Talking and Listening

Proverbs 17:27—
"One who spares words is knowledgeable; / one who is cool in spirit has understanding."

• Reflective Listening

God gives us two ears and only one mouth. Perhaps this indicates that we should listen twice as much as we talk. In reality, most parents do far more talking than listening. Good communication skills must be nurtured and practiced. Starting when children are very young, listen to their spoken thoughts, encourage their conversational skills. When adolescence strikes, parents wonder why their children refuse to talk to them. Although this is typical behavior for the age, if a habit of communicating was developed throughout childhood, children are more likely to continue sharing with caring parents.

Give children your full attention. Get on eye level with them. At a communication workshop the instructor paired us off, making one person stand on a chair. We were then required to carry on a conversation. After a few minutes we switched positions. Looking up constantly as we were talking was difficult and intimidating. The person on the chair held the power, a sense of authority. This exercise provided us with a vivid example of what life is like for children.

Make physical contact while talking. Hold children's hands, or place your hand on their shoulder. Look directly at them, proving they have your attention. This skill is especially helpful when disciplining, showing loving concern, breaking down any confrontational atmosphere.

As you listen to what children are telling you, try to understand any underlying problem. When they have finished, state what you think you heard, and ask if that was what they meant to say. If you did not get the right message, perhaps they can restate the situation so you can better understand. Repeat the procedure.

Reflective listening means the parent becomes a mirror, simply reflecting back to the child what the parent is hearing (in words) and seeing (in body language). Developing children's ability to think about their words and actions gives them increased impulse control in situations. Children learn to think about what is going on and plan a course of action—skills that will benefit them throughout life.

• Finding the Words

Helping children find the appropriate words to describe situations and concerns is another parental responsibility. Keep in mind that preschool children have very limited vocabularies, only 700 words at three years of age. Often feelings they are experiencing are beyond their verbal skills. With reflective listening techniques, parents can explain new words to children and help them understand new concepts. Although time consuming, the resulting increase in communication ability rewards the effort.

Do not give up if children become frustrated trying to share feelings about an incident. Often my daughter would throw up her hands, tell me I just didn't understand, and go to her room. Oh well, I tried to use the "right technique," and hoped she knew that I was interested and concerned, yet unwilling to try to solve her problems for her. My task was to help her understand her feelings.

Speaking of describing feelings, acknowledging and affirming feelings is essential. God gives us our emotions as part of our human composition. Feelings are not good or bad, they just ARE! How a person acts on those feelings determines appropriate or inappropriate behavior. Accept what children are feeling. Never tell them they should *not* feel that way. They cannot help what they are feeling. If they are not allowed to express the feelings verbally, they may act them out physically, or bottle them up inside. Psychologists find the bottling up of emotions destructive, requiring long hours of therapy to help people learn to open up to their feelings.

When my husband and I attended Marriage Encounter, we found that putting our feelings into words was the most difficult exercise of the experience. Here is a list of some words that describe feelings. How would you put these feelings into words a child would understand? There are more human emotions than happy, sad, and angry. Try these: proud, mischievous, scared, worried, secure, disappointed, envious, playful, enraged, jealous, confused, crabby, remorseful, determined, optimistic, lonely, shy, excited, hurt, sorry, silly, loved. Start expanding your emotional vocabulary.

When you parents are experiencing strong emotions, share them with the children. Put into words the feelings you are having in order to help them learn about our human emotions. Aid them in becoming compassionate.

• **Problem-Solving Skills**

Helping children develop the ability to solve problems ranks with the most important life skills. When faced with a dilemma, children must learn how to think through the possibilities, reaching a satisfactory conclusion on their own. Parents will not always be around to help children make decisions. All parents want their children to make good decisions. Do not solve children's problems for them. Be a sounding board. Let them describe the problem. Ask how they could handle the situation. Brainstorm for many possible solutions. Look at the consequence of each solution until children are satisfied with a plan of action.

If a child is having a problem with a classmate, one solution might be a knock-down-drag-out fight. This would result in punishment by school officials, if not physical injury. Other solutions might include: telling the other child verbally what the problem appears to be, and asking that child for any solutions he or she might have for the situation; asking the teacher or parents to become involved, which might result in more teasing from classmates; ignoring the problem classmate, and concentrating on making other friends; changing schools, thus losing all current friends. Look at all the possibilities, even the extreme ones. Teaching problem-solving skills requires making choices.

Children who are always told what to do, how to act, and what to say, never develop the confidence to act on their own. Instilling self-confidence should be a high priority for every parent. When children make decisions, do not criticize the choice. That destroys their burgeoning confidence. Encourage them to discuss how they came to the decision and what consequences occurred. Find out their feelings about the outcome. Foster reflection on the situation and how they might handle the problem if it arises again. Ask what they have learned from the experience.

The Systematic Training for Effective Parenting series (see Appendix 1) devotes a lot of discussion to looking at behavior problems and deciding whose problem it is to solve. As parents, we tend to take on too much responsibility. If a situation directly affects a parent's life, then it is the parent's problem. If the situation directly affects the child's life, it is the child's problem. Unless the child's health or safety is involved, the parent should enable the child to work out a solution to the problem. If a child is not ready for school in the morning, that is the child's problem. The child suffers the consequences of being late. When the child's tardiness makes the parent late for work, however, it then becomes the parent's problem to solve.

Discussion Questions

1. Role play with another person. Practice reflective listening. Scenario: You have been unfairly reprimanded by a supervisor for an error on a report. You had received incorrect input. You are telling your spouse about the incident.

2. Pretend you are four years old and your parents have just brought home a new baby, your first sibling. Describe possible feelings.

3. Problem: Your best friend dumped you and joined the popular crowd at school. They point at you, whisper, and laugh. You are miserable! Brainstorm for possible solutions.

Chapter 10

Interaction

Ephesians 4:31–32—
"Put away from you all bitterness and wrath and anger and wrangling and slander, together with all malice, and be kind to one another, tenderhearted, forgiving one another, as God in Christ has forgiven you."

• Conflict Resolution

No form of abuse should be tolerated in the home. A child's home should be a safe haven from the stresses of the world. Verbal and emotional abuse are as damaging as physical and sexual abuse. Demeaning, shaming, and neglecting children do not get as much publicity, however. Self-esteem, once destroyed, becomes difficult to reestablish.

Within family life, conflict between members, especially siblings, becomes a most disruptive force. Teaching children appropriate ways to handle conflict must start with never allowing physical violence in the home. Domestic violence gets much attention as society seemingly becomes more violence prone. Now, even in preschools, children are being taught to use words, not fists (or knives and guns) to solve disputes. Looking for win-win situations in which there is no "loser" remains paramount. Consequences for unacceptable behavior should be established and consistently enforced. *Consistent* is the key word. Rules haphazardly enforced lose all effectiveness.

Media portray violence as the solution to problems so frequently that children have become conditioned to respond similarly. Because they witness so much killing on television, usually without seeing the results on grieving families, plus the fact that the actors are back on television the next day, the reality of death is abstract. Teaching peaceful solutions has become an uphill battle for parents and teachers.

Step one: limit the amount of television children view. Step two: eliminate violent programming and movies. Parents are in charge and responsible for what children learn. When watching a program with your children, if something inappropriate is portrayed, talk with the children about the value of human life and the dignity of each person. Fill in some of the details the media leave out.

Inordinate amounts of television viewing reduce communication skills in general. Testing of vocabulary among high school students shows a continual decline in these skills. Families need to spend time talking together about world issues. At mealtime especially, turn off the television and talk to the children.

Mention needs to be made here of teaching children about forgiveness. Forcing a child to say "I'm sorry" does not solve disputes. Realization of the effects of an action must be explained and comprehended. Some type of restitution should be made, depending on the behavior that occurred. When ready to acknowledge the offense, step one is to ask for forgiveness from the offended person. After the other party forgives, step two would be to ask if anything could be done to demonstrate the sincerity of the apology, such as a change in behavior. Step three is to forgive yourself for causing harm. This is often the hardest step of all, especially for adults.

Do you see the sacrament of reconciliation in these steps? Children can only learn about God's forgiveness if it is modeled in the home. At parenting presentations, we stress the need for parents to be willing to ask for their children's forgiveness when they have erred against the children. Parents can model God's forgiveness when forgiving children for offenses by not bringing the matter up over and over again. Let "forgive and *forget*" become a reality.

At one presentation, a grandmotherly woman questioned the need to apologize to one's children. She had never, not once in her life, admitted she was wrong to her children because she felt it would lessen her position of authority in their eyes. What does this teach children about forgiveness, especially God's forgiveness? We are human. We make mistakes. Do not set yourself up as being perfect. You will be heading for a fall from that pedestal. We all need to be forgiven at times. Teach your children the joy of being forgiving, as well as being forgiven. You are "God with skin on" to your children. Children experience God's unconditional love through the actions of parents and adults who love them—an awesome responsibility!

• Family Meetings

Since mealtime should be kept enjoyable and pleasant, a time to learn communication skills, it is not the appropriate time to bring up family issues and disputes. Establish regularly scheduled family meetings, at least monthly, if not weekly, to deal with family business. Run the meeting like a business meeting; after all, a family is like a small business. Rotate the person in charge of the meeting. Have that person create an agenda of issues to be discussed. Family members can submit items for discussion.

When household rules are set up in a cooperative manner, family members tend to be more compliant. Keep the number of family rules to a minimum, covering only the most important issues. Discuss each family member's rights and responsibilities. Let the children help develop consequences for breaking rules. Parents often must intercede because children tend to make punishments more severe than necessary. Write down the agreed-upon rules, posting them in a prominent location so that family members are constantly aware of the rules. Keep the rules updated. Needs of a family change. Enforce the rules or they become meaningless.

Certain basic rules of every home should be: no physical violence, no abusive or foul language, no ridicule or malicious teasing, no taking others' possessions without permission. Consequences for violations should be agreed upon in advance so no family member can use the excuse of not knowing. After basic rules, families decide what particular problems need addressing in their home, and what appropriate consequences will be.

At family meetings household chores can be assigned, duties redistributed and negotiated. Budget concerns, family expenses, and allowances can be discussed. Family vacation plans can be evaluated, researched, and reported on. Upcoming celebrations can be planned together as a family. The more that children can be involved in family decision making, the more important they feel, and the more secure they become as valued members of the family team.

Try to plan the family meetings at a time when all family members can be present. Open the meeting with a prayer. One member of the family can be in charge of the prayer. Keep the meetings short. Follow the agenda. Close with a special treat. A different family member can be in charge of the food and/or drink. Make this family event a time everyone looks forward to attending.

• Television Affects Interaction

During a presentation by John F. Kavanaugh, S.J., author of *Following Christ in a Consumer Society*, many ads were shown promoting conspicuous consumption. One that stuck with me portrayed a family sitting around a living room, all with their own small, personal television on their lap. The ad proclaimed "Peace on Earth." I remain horrified to this day. They weren't communicating with each other. They all seemed happy in their own world. Many families go a step further: each person is in his/her *own room* with his/her *own television*, plus cable box and video recorder. If family members do not spend time interacting, the value of family is further diminished. Be aware of television's effect on your family (along with computers and video games). Limit "screen" time.

Observing young children at play while a television is on as background noise illustrates an interesting fact about the role television plays in daily life. Children play contentedly, until a commercial comes on. They then turn toward the sound, transfixed, hypnotized by the music and action. When the commercial ends, they return to their play, until the next commercial. What parents fail to realize is that commercials are the whole point of television programming. The programs are developed to bring an audience to the advertisers. More money is spent on commercials than on programming. The best minds in advertising are utilized in creating spots that will attract the attention of children and teens. Memorable jingles and name recognition are two goals, along with creating need for the product. The purpose of television is to sell. Children and teens control a tremendous portion of spendable income in our economy, and are an important *target audience*.

Media literacy (see Appendix 2), a long neglected area, is making strides in raising awareness of deceptive practices in advertising. Parents need to educate themselves about the effects of television in order to help their children develop the skills necessary to avoid becoming victims of unscrupulous advertisers. Because of an inability to think abstractly, young children have difficulty in separating fantasy from reality. What they see on television is all very real to them. They are concrete thinkers. They expect advertising promises to be kept. Reality, especially with toys and food items, is a source of much disappointment. Therefore, limit children's exposure to TV viewing.

Use a video recorder to record programs of interest and benefit that may be scheduled at inconvenient times. With video tapes you can fast forward past the commercials. Watching television with your children provides many opportunities for teachable moments. Parents can analyze both the commercials and the programs with children, pointing out special effects used to create illusions. If values contrary to family ethics are portrayed, parents need to be there to be the voice that speaks out against contrary values. Ask yourself, "Would I invite a person with this lifestyle or value system into my home?" If the answer is no, then don't. Turn the television off!

We always tried to supervise what the children watched. One evening I picked up a video recommended by a friend. My daughter was about ten years old and deeply involved in ballet, tap, and jazz dancing. The title, "Dirty Dancing," should have been enough clue. As the movie progressed, my husband asked who had recommended the film. The film led to discussions about abortion, inappropriate teenage behavior, and casual sexual activity. Our teenage son went to his room, saying our moralizing was ruining the movie. We could have turned the movie off, but we knew that many of her classmates had already seen it. We preferred to give her our input on the morality of the situations portrayed.

Mentioning this incident at a presentation to parents, a woman responded that the daycare center where she works uses that particular video often. The preschoolers love the dance sequences. When questioned about the scenes of sexual activity, she replied that the participants were covered by sheets. She believed that those themes went over the preschoolers' heads. Wake up! Children, like sponges, absorb everything they see and hear. There are definitely more appropriate videos for children to watch.

Children need to be directed toward educational programming. They will not necessarily seek it out. An advantage we had when our boys were young was that we only had one television in the house. My husband retained control of the "remote," therefore controlling what was being viewed in the evening. If the boys finished their homework and wanted to watch television, they had to negotiate with their father. They learned to enjoy public television broadcasts. To this day, they enjoy educational television. Their wives cannot believe their avid interest in such programs. I attribute it to their exposure during the formative, early years. Both "boys" have scientific, inquisitive, analytic minds, each earning a Ph.D. in his field.

Beware of the habit of turning the television on mindlessly; only turn it on with the purpose of watching a particular program. Hours can dwindle away while we sit mesmerized by pointless programming. Be watchful of how you spend your TIME! Use television as a tool to *enhance* family communication, not destroy it.

Discussion Questions

1. Practice negotiating skills to resolve this conflict: your teenager wants to attend a rock concert with friends, but you do not approve of the songs' lyrics.

2. Set up an agenda for a one-hour family meeting, including prayer and snack. Select three topics for discussion and create one new family rule from the discussion.

3. Think about the last television show you watched in its entirety with your children. How did you utilize "teachable moments?"

Chapter 11

Management

Proverbs 13:20—
"Whoever walks with the wise becomes wise, but the companion of fools suffers harm."

• TIME Management Skills

Two crucial areas for families to practice management skills are TIME and MONEY. Whatever skills family members have acquired in the workplace need to be applied to the home. Using a day planner to keep track of family activities becomes essential when several schedules need to be meshed.

With three children all going in different directions, I remember being so rattled at one point that I would sometimes miss doctor and dentist appointments. Finally, in desperation, I bought a large dry-erase white-board that was partitioned off in thirty-five squares, enabling me to record a month's activity at a time. I placed it on the wall coming in from the garage, so all family members would see it daily. They were responsible to write down and change any of their activities for the current month. When we put up a new month's calendar, everybody wrote down his or her input. Lon and I still use the same system.

During a time management seminar, I learned to prioritize daily activities. This skill can make each day more productive.

The instructors suggest waking up fifteen minutes earlier each morning, then brainstorming all the items that need to be handled that day—in detail. Then they suggest that, after listing items on a tablet kept beside the bed, we go through and mark the most important as "A": must be accomplished; then assign "B" items: will hopefully get done; and finally the "C" items: get to if all "A" and "B" items are completed. As you go through the day, do the "A" items first. You get a real feeling of accomplishment as you cross off the items. Then move on to the "B" items. At the end of the day, review the list, feel pride in all that was accomplished. Items remaining go to tomorrow's list, perhaps moving up from "C" to "B"![12]

At another time management workshop, the educator had a stopwatch and timed one minute for the participants. She said that although it seems like so little time, each minute counts. She started listing all the things a person could accomplish in one minute. Being organized to do small tasks is what counts. Keep bills, notepaper, and stamps by the phone for times you are put on hold. Have some stationery in the car to write quick thank-you notes while waiting for children. Put a couple of cookbooks and some notepaper in the car; do menu planning and grocery lists in waiting rooms. Make every minute count.

She also spoke of time wasted in telephone conversations. She kept a fake doorbell by her phone, and when she wanted to end a conversation she rang it and excused herself to "get the door." Another helpful tip I have used extensively: you do not have to make excuses to telephone solicitors. They are infringing on *your* time. You need not be overly polite. Just a quick "Not interested!" will do. We now let the answering machine handle these irritating mealtime interruptions. A minute saved is a minute to be spent in a more fulfilling way.

• Using TIME Wisely

Enlist the help of family members. Depending on their ages, give children responsibilities to ease the load. Find ways they can accomplish tasks successfully. Buy some plastic plates at a discount store, so they can set the table when they are young. Teach them how to dust, but put valuable objects out of reach until children are older. Combine tasks. Wipe down the bathroom while supervising bath time. Fold a load of clothes while listening to a child read to you. Teach children to sort socks and underwear, fold clothes and towels. Plan shopping outings with a list of goals, then nothing is forgotten and the trip is mapped out more efficiently.

As children get older, their task assignments can become more challenging. In the evening they can lay out clothes for morning, make their own lunches, set the table for breakfast, organize backpacks and homework, find shoes (and any miscellaneous sports equipment that will be needed the next day). In the morning, dirty clothes go into a hamper, bed gets straightened, everyone's dressed, breakfast is eaten, and they're out the door. Sound good?

Spending time searching for lost items always seemed to be a problem around our house. Out of desperation, I instituted "a place for everything and everything in its place" program. Organization of belongings not only saves time, but becomes a skill that will help children throughout life. Make them responsible to put things where they belong. Build shelves, get boxes or tubs, give each child a desk or dresser where he or she can keep personal items. Teach children to be responsible for their space and their belongings.

Dinnertime, especially for parents working outside the home, can become a test of patience. Try over the weekend to plan meals for the week. Get suggestions from all family members. Purchase necessary ingredients. Make dishes ahead of time for quick reheating. Double the recipe and freeze half for another dinner. Make salad for the week, putting it in an airtight container. (Keep tomatoes, mushrooms, cucumbers, and other soggy items separate from the lettuce.) Soups and stews can be made in large quantity and served up quickly. Crockpots fill homes with wonderful aromas.

Letting family members participate in the cooking process not only teaches important life skills, but also provides quantity time together that often results in quality time (if you do not lose your patience). My daughter has always loved the kitchen. She and I work together quite often. I am in charge of assembling ingredients and providing clean-up as we progress. She likes vegetarian foods. We teach each other many things.

When my son moved into his first apartment, he would call home to find out how to make particular dishes that he liked. He was into sports while growing up, not cooking. He learned cooking skills as they were needed. Now he watches cooking programs on television and has become a very creative cook. His wife had not learned cooking skills while young either, so they work together creating meals. Their teamwork is impressive.

Remember that involving children in household responsibilities not only gives parents needed help, it empowers children to feel capable, which builds self-esteem. Although it may take extra time at first while teaching a skill, the rewards will be worth the trouble.

At a confirmation weekend retreat, my team of girls was assigned (by lottery draw) clean up of the women's restroom and showers. My team had a fit! The girls especially were not going to clean toilets! When I asked them what they planned to do when they had their own homes, they responded, "Hire someone to clean!" I hated to bust their bubble, but life doesn't always work that way. Eventually they put on the rubber gloves and got busy cleaning.

• Financial Management

Economic expectations were discussed in Chapter 6, dealing with the financial situation in which a person is raised. Financial planning and management needs to be a day-to-day conscious effort to reach set goals. Many marriages are damaged, if not destroyed, by financial disagreements and woes.

A family is a business. It needs to be run on the same economic principles as a business. Income and expenses need careful examination and evaluation. Savings goals should be established with an eye toward vacations, home purchase, medical/dental expenses, automotive repairs and maintenance, college costs, and retirement.

Couples need to be aware of the cost of raising a family and prepare for the expenses, so as not to be caught unaware. The USDA Family Economics Research Group released figures in 1991 showing the cost of raising a child born in 1990 to the age of seventeen to be $210,070 for a middle income family. This takes into account housing, food, clothing, insurance, medical/dental, transportation, and the million and one "little things" children require. These figures do not include tuitions to private schools and items such as music/dance lessons or sports training.

The complete concept can seem overwhelming. Is it any wonder young adults delay moving out on their own and accepting the responsibility and commitment of marriage and family? Thus the current trend of returning to parents' homes when life gets too expensive. Have parents planned on supporting grown children? Does a retirement income allow for these additional expenses?

Examine the cost of using credit. Credit card companies make it too easy for people to get into debt, especially college students. My children were issued credit cards as college freshmen. They had no credit rating, no full-time employment history. In

1990 credit card companies removed the requirement for students to have cosigners. Since then, credit card debt has plagued college students and many working young adults. Before they realize what is happening they are in financial trouble because of the freedom to "charge it." Many look to parents for a bail-out.

An article appearing in the *Los Angeles Times* on January 23, 2001, reported that the percentage of bankruptcies filed for persons under twenty-five years of age increased from 1% in 1996 to 5% in 1998. The filings this year are estimated to exceed 150,000 for young adults. Easy credit, consumerism, inability to delay gratification, and lack of schooling in financial management all contribute to the problem.

Teaching children the value of money early in life through the effective use of allowances and budgets allows them to cope better with financial management in the future. Learning responsible saving and spending habits will strengthen them against pressures that might lure them into debt and disaster.

A helpful book, *A Penny Saved,* is an easy-to-understand guide to teaching children money management skills that will benefit them throughout life. Discussion is divided into preschool, grade school age, and teenage sections. No matter what age children are, parents can begin financial training. Plans are quite detailed, allowing families to choose a plan that works for them.

> Teaching your kids to have a good grasp on the financial realities is one of the best ways of preparing them to deal with all the unexpected changes life will send their way. Life isn't fair. We all know that, yet it's still a shock every time we're confronted by its unfairness—we need to be solidly grounded so that we're not emotionally devastated.[13]

Discussion Questions

1. Take a few minutes to think about what things need to be accomplished tomorrow. Make a list of *everything*, then prioritize the items as A, B, or C.

2. Make a menu plan for one week, taking into account the food preferences of all family members. How could all family members help with mealtimes?

3. Depending on the age of your children, calculate a weekly allowance amount that would cover their expenses and teach financial planning. List expenses and goals. Remember to take into account savings and charitable contributions.

Chapter 12

Encouragement

Proverbs 15:23—
"To make an apt answer is a joy to anyone, and a word in season, how good it is!"

• Parents as Cheerleaders

Life holds so much to learn and master. Children have a lifetime of learning ahead of them. They need strong role models, knowledgeable instructors, compassionate friends, but most of all some enthusiastic cheerleaders. The responsibility of cheerleaders at any sporting event is to encourage the team toward victory, to keep hope alive, to inspire maximum effort.

Encouragement to meet life's challenges, take risks, experience new adventures, should come from those closest to children—parents. A "you can do it" attitude shows confidence in children's ability to at least try. If children do not succeed in first attempts, encouragement helps them realize that trying was the most important part. Then children have confidence to try again without fear of being shamed.

Praise and encouragement are very different. Praise teaches children that they have pleased the adult. Encouragement aims at teaching children to be proud of themselves and their accomplishments. Encouragement notices effort and improvement. The danger with too much praise is that children come to rely on it for self-worth. When praise is not given, those children feel unappreciated. Praise becomes a reward in itself. Children come to rely on praise as motivation. If they fear failure they may not try because there is no praise for failure.

Being responsible cheerleaders, parents must continue to cheer even when the team is losing. Fostering hope for future improvement keeps the team fired up and players giving their best effort. Notice small efforts and improvements; do not dwell on failures. Remember that at the game's end, no matter what the score, cheerleaders continue cheering as the team leaves the playing field.

Encouragement lets children know that you love them for who they are, not what they accomplish. This allows children to enjoy life, escaping the pressures of having to be "the best." Appreciating efforts and asking children if *they* are enjoying the experience of activities undertaken remain the primary tasks of "cheerleaders." The Systematic Training for Effective Parenting series (see Appendix 1) contains extensive discussions on encouragement at three developmental levels—early childhood, grade school age, and teenager.

• Creating Lovable/Capable Children

Two main goals of parents should be to help their children become lovable and capable. Lovable children have learned manners and are well disciplined; they have been taught the rules of socially acceptable behavior. Unruly children refuse to follow rules or social guidelines, resulting in exclusion by playmates and adults. Friendships and acceptance are key elements of children's growing self-esteem. If a child bullies others to get attention, most likely that child will not be well liked. He or she may only be able to attract others who behave similarly.

Encouragement

The opinion adults hold of children builds self-esteem, even though children will not readily admit that they care what adults think of them. Teaching children to greet adults, shake hands, say please and thank you, all contribute to a child's social standing. Taking turns, sharing, being concerned for the welfare of others, are life skills that will help children cope throughout life.

Wanting to be accepted by others and have friends is part of our human nature. When children are not taught the skills necessary to achieve these goals, they often react in negative, destructive ways. Adults who deal with children, especially teachers, emphasize the importance of a child's polite social behavior in both peer acceptance and gaining respect from adults. Give children the advantage of good manners.

Capable children exude confidence that they can accomplish tasks and reach goals. They have been encouraged to make efforts to learn skills, and are willing to take risks in meeting new challenges. Such children have been given responsibilities and developed pride in their own abilities. Start teaching life skills during the early childhood years.

Young children learn to be organized by being responsible for returning their personal items to the proper place. Responsibilities like setting and clearing the table can be taught by using plastic dishes when children are young. Dusting can be mastered, even use of a vacuum cleaner. A bed consisting of a fitted bottom sheet and a comforter is easy for young children to make up. Help can even be had in the sorting and folding of laundry. When they went away to college my children appreciated that I had taught them how to do their own laundry. They had to teach their fellow students.

A word of caution—a friend was so impressed that my children did their own laundry that she decided to teach her teenage son how to do wash. After successfully accomplishing the training, she told him that since she was now working full time, she was willing to pay him for each load he washed, dried, folded, and put away. She would sort the laundry in piles for him. He got so enterprising that one day he searched the house for more wash, to earn more money. He threw her navy blue linen suit, which was set aside for the dry cleaners, into the washer, along with some of his sisters' clothing. Not good! An expensive lesson for everyone. Back to giving specific, detailed instructions (and limits). Teach them also to read washing-instruction labels!

The more things children learn to do well, the stronger their self-esteem. They see themselves as an asset to the family team. Look for jobs that children can accomplish successfully, and start young. In *Life in the Family Zoo,* John Platt talks about parents missing the golden years—when children *want* to help. When children are young, parents often find it easier to do tasks themselves than supervise children doing tasks, so they send the children out to play. When children get to be eight years old, parents suddenly realize the children have no responsibilities. What is the first task parents usually assign children? Right—take out the trash. Dr. Platt thinks such a task does not really build up a person's self-worth. Find tasks with more affirming potential. His humorous approach lightens the task of parenting.[14]

Let children help. Show appreciation. Remove the word *but* from your parenting vocabulary. That one small word can destroy a message that parents intended to be encouraging. For instance, saying "I appreciate the way you picked up your toys, *but* you left the books on the floor," negates the affirmation that came before the word *but*. Children tend to remember only the criticism, and that is how they view the "but message." Their efforts are never good enough.

Sometimes parents need to adjust their expectations, lower their standards, and accept best efforts. Another of my wall plaque collection reminds me: "Our home is clean enough to be healthy, but dirty enough to be happy." Of course, when our home was burglarized and the police came to take a report, they did ask why our son's room was the only one ransacked. We had to admit that it always looked that way. He has improved since his adolescent years, his wife now sees to that.

• Natural/Logical Consequences

Being a child often means feeling powerless, with others constantly telling you what to do and when to do it. Choices are seldom the child's to make. How then do children learn to make good choices? They need practice in both making choices and living with the consequences of the choices made. Responsibility is thus learned.

Parents assist children in becoming mature by enabling them to make choices and decisions, even as preschoolers. In a child-development class, the professor said parents should let their children pick out their own clothes for school from the early years onward. An uproar ensued from mothers in the class who felt they would be humiliated by their children's choice in clothing. The professor recommended at least giving young children "limited choices," between two outfits, thus satisfying everyone's needs and empowering the child. I silently thanked God for Catholic school uniforms. Of course, when taking my eighth-grade son shopping for "graduation party" clothes, he replied to the sales clerk's inquiry as to his favorite style, "I go to Catholic school, I have no style!" This might be considered a drawback.

Learning to live with the consequences of behavior is a necessary part of becoming a responsible, mature person. Natural consequences occur all the time. Parents do not have to be involved; in fact, they should not be involved. When parents intervene, not allowing natural consequences, lessons are not learned. Simple things, like forgetting your lunch (you go hungry), leaving your homework at home (your grade is lowered), or oversleeping and being late to school (you get detention), teach a child to be more responsible the next time. The more that parents bail their children out of predicaments, the more irresponsible children become. When they are on their own and working for an employer, there will be no bail-outs. Detaching is difficult, but necessary.

When we went to college orientation with our oldest son, a parent at the "dorm living" session asked if the dorms provided wake-up calls. When the Resident Advisor regained control and ceased laughing, he replied, "This is not a hotel!" Personal responsibility is one of the most important life lessons children need to master.

After my daughter turned sixteen, she began driving herself to school. Each morning followed the same pattern with *me* waking her up, *me* reminding her of the time passing, *me* asking what she wanted in her lunch, *me* trying to get her to eat breakfast. We would both be upset before she left the house. I wondered how she would ever survive college without *me*! Finally I let go, staying in bed until she was gone. Sometimes she was late and had detention, but that was *her responsibility*. If she could not get to sport or play practice because of detention, that too was *her problem*. Turning over responsibility is very freeing to parents. By the way, she not only survived college on the East Coast, but thrived on her own.

Logical consequences require a great deal more thought and practice. Going through the training workshops for Systematic Training for Effective Parenting (see Appendix 1) gives parents valuable experience and guidance. Mainly, the goal is to tie the consequence to the misbehavior. Lessons may not be learned if the child does not see the connection between the action and the resulting "punishment," preferably referred to as "consequence."

For instance, if a child rides her bicycle in the street, or goes on her bike where she was not supposed to go, taking the bicycle away for a specific period of time is a *logical consequence*. The child did not behave *responsibly* with the bicycle. The child made a bad choice. The child will be allowed to try again in one week to be more responsible with her bike. The second time this particular irresponsible behavior occurs, the elapsed time before another attempt to act responsibly increases. If the parent said no television for two weeks, as *punishment*, the child would not see the logical connection.

If the child cannot get up in the morning or has missing homework assignments because of watching television, then no television would be a logical consequence for that behavior. Thinking up logical consequences becomes a real challenge for parents, but then again, good parenting is always challenging. Nobody gets it all right all the time! I was told about a creative principal who cured students of doing spitballs by making those students caught fill a paper cup with spitballs, since they apparently needed to chew paper! It does take some creative thought, so plan ahead.

Thankfully, God knows we are trying our human best to raise responsible, lovable, capable, caring children. Rely on God's help during difficult times. Pray, pour your heart out, then listen carefully. God may be sending you inspirations and creative ideas that you are failing to pick up due to your faulty receiver. Give yourself a spiritual tuneup.

Discussion Questions

1. Your child is working on a school science project. Think up some encouraging statements, as opposed to praise.

2. Make a list of ways each child in the family contributes to the smooth functioning of family life.

3. Create a list of logical consequences for the misbehavior of a child not turning in school assignments.

Section 4

Making TIME to Develop Parenting Skills

Chapter 13

Togetherness

Proverbs 29:17—
"Discipline your children and they will give you rest; /
they will give delight to your heart."

• Agree on Parenting Techniques

Parents need to be in agreement on the methods of parenting they will follow. Having one strict, authoritarian parent and one who believes in a more democratic approach to parenting spells disaster. Thoughtful discussion of issues needs to result in agreement by compromise. Search for win-win situations in which everyone's needs are met.

Consistency in discipline establishes guidelines children can learn and follow. If a parent says no to a request a dozen times, then relents and says yes, the child learns that pestering succeeds. Next time the child will continue hounding the parent until he or she succeeds in getting another yes. Say no only when you really mean no. If there is a chance you might change your mind, give a milder response, such as, "We'll see." Save those "no" responses for really important issues on which you will not reverse a previous decision. If you give in once, it takes holding the line ten times to reestablish your credibility when the answer is no.

Make rules you are willing to enforce *consistently.* Rules without consequences become meaningless. Keep rules to a minimum and only regarding serious matters. As was discussed previously, establish rules and consequences at family meetings with a consensus of opinion. Children are more likely to comply if they have helped make up the rules. Write rules down and post them in a prominent location. Give children as much trust and freedom as they are developmentally ready to handle. Pull freedoms back if they behave irresponsibly.

If children find that they can go from one parent to the other, getting different answers to requests, not only do they become confused, this undermines both parents' authority. Also, children's sense of security is shaken when they witness parents in disagreement over discipline matters. Parents' trust in each other weakens when they fail to back up each other's decisions. Use the tried and true: "I will talk it over with your mother/father and get back to you on that matter."

• Communication Is Key

Not only must parents learn to discuss issues together, they must find the time and privacy to hold such discussions. When our boys were young, we felt as though we were losing touch with each other. Agreeing that we needed more couple time, we arranged to have a teenage girl babysit every Thursday evening for three hours, six to nine. We agreed to pay her every Thursday whether we used her or not. Therefore she kept the date open for us, and we felt more compelled to get out of the house. We even ended up taking a photography course together for one semester. It was great.

As the children got older and schedules became even more hectic, we came up with a different plan. Lon and I went to six-thirty Mass one morning a week, then stopped for a doughnut and coffee. The children were warned that they were responsible to get themselves out of bed, dressed, and breakfast eaten. We would be home in time to check on their progress and drive car pool. We had some private time, and they learned to be responsible for themselves. Everyone benefited.

Set aside some small slot of time for the two of you. If there are going to be disagreements on parenting issues, better to hash them out while walking at a park, taking a drive, or over a cup of coffee, than in front of the children. Negotiation and communication skills require years of practice and *concentration*.

There are some general guidelines that help couples grow together through conflict. Since most disagreements are really about wanting to be heard, listen to each other and validate one another's opinion. Stick to the subject under discussion, one issue at a time, and no dumping hurts of the past into the discussion. Watch your words and tone of voice. Would you talk this way to your best friend? Talk about feelings underlying the issue. Explore the wide variety of emotions human beings are capable of having. Look for ways to compromise, be generous, give in to the other sometimes. Remember, it should be more important to be married than to be right all the time. Be sure the issue gets resolved; don't leave it to fester.

Remember that very few people, if any, possess the ability to read minds. Often we think we know what the other person is thinking. Most likely, we are wrong. When upset, people create scenarios in their mind that are far from the reality of the situation. As the old adage says: ASSUME makes an ASS out of U and ME. Talk it out.

• Remember Why You Two Married

Whatever you do, do not lose touch with each other. In the hectic pace of daily living, neglecting the couple relationship is all too easy. From the time the first child is born, husbands feel displaced. Wives' attention becomes focused almost exclusively on the newborn. Husbands need to recognize this as nature's way of insuring the survival of the species. Wives need to be inclusive of the new daddy, so he feels that he plays an important role also.

Do special little things for one another to keep romance alive. Tuck notes into briefcases and lunch sacks. Send an e-mail that says, "I am glad we are married." Try to make one day a month special for the two of you. A spiritual director advised me to make the special date the day of our wedding, on the twenty-second of the month. Send a mushy card to your spouse's workplace. Leave an "I Love You" phone message. Make a special meal. Set a candle-lit table. Put the kids to bed early. Dance to a favorite song. Watch a romantic movie. Renew your wedding vows.

Sharing responsibilities should deepen the couple relationship. Marriage is not a fifty-fifty proposition! It's is a ninety-ten proposition for both parties. When one parent is stressed, the other may be called upon to carry more responsibility. Give-and-take keeps one parent from becoming overwhelmed, deepening love's roots and holding the couple secure through life's storms. If there is work stress, share what is happening, then the other party can be compassionate. Being grouchy and short-tempered just meets with retaliation.

A few reminders of ways to keep your marriage alive and well: keep talking, communication is essential; treasure your spouse; they are giving their life to you; face life as friends; never stop courting; be committed to your marriage, divorce is not in your vocabulary; laugh a lot, be silly; get professional help when needed; listen to advice with openness.

There are always periods in our lives when we are under extreme pressure, more stressed than usual. Keep a perspective that things will improve and that this is a temporary problem.

Turn to God for added help and inspiration. Lift up the concerns of your heart. Give them to God for resolution, remembering that God's answers are not always the answers we want to hear. Listen with an open heart and trust God.

Discussion Questions

1. Your teenager wants to spend spring break with friends at a vacation spot. Work out an agreement between one strict parent and one permissive parent.

2. Discuss the last time you and your spouse were able to hold an uninterrupted half hour conversation about a parenting issue. What were the results?

3. Separately plan a romantic evening for the two of you, on paper. What would be included? Compare your ideas. Work out a plan, and do it.

Chapter 14

Intimacy

Proverbs 31:10–12—
"A capable wife who can find? / She is far more precious than jewels. / The heart of her husband trusts in her, / and he will have no lack of gain. / She does him good, and not harm, / all the days of her life."

• Parents as Sexual Role Models

Children need to know that their parents are in love. The security they feel from witnessing expressions of physical affection, such as hand-holding, hugging, and kissing, models to children healthy sexual behavior. Modern media seldom portray married couples being affectionate and loving. Too often ma*rital* relationships are depicted more as ma*rtial* relationships: confrontational, degrading, the punch line for humor.

Once while I was watching a television news magazine broadcast exploring teenage sexuality, teens revealed their attitudes and behaviors. Popular thinking among teens was that kissing is necessarily the prelude to sexual intercourse. The two are irrevocably linked. You cannot engage in the first without the other happening. That is how they see life. Has media contributed to this thinking? To what degree? Watch MTV for a while and you will get your answer.

Children need to learn that affectionate behaviors can exist on their own, without necessarily leading into deeper sexual intimacy. Kissing, hugging, and holding hands can be wonderful in their own right. Someone must teach children when and where to draw boundaries and distinctions. It will definitely not be the media that do this task for us. Parents need to take more active roles in educating children from the early years on respecting their bodies and the bodies of others.

Another aspect of intimacy on which teens need to be educated is the distinction between love and infatuation. When hormones start raging, teens, especially girls, may think they are "in love." What they really are is infatuated. Parents need to model to their children deep, lasting, committed love. Infatuation usually is a quickly occurring physical attraction that overlooks faults and sees the object of infatuation as "perfect." Many times friends and relatives dislike the relationship, but that fuels the feeling of being in love and against the world. The biggest danger of infatuation is premature sexual activity which can result in pregnancy, sexually transmitted disease, and even death. These issues must be talked about realistically in today's world. These are natural consequences. Distance and quarreling cool infatuation, whereas real love deepens with time, quarreling lessens, and distance strengthens resolve. The extreme ups and downs, highs and lows, of infatuation, or "puppy love," take a toll on parents, but patience and good example are the best ways to teach children about true love.[15]

• Parental Privacy Essential

Most teenagers believe that their parents are no longer sexually active. Even the thought of their parents "doing it" grosses teens out. Media tend to propagate the notion that the only "good sex" occurs between unmarried persons. Is it any wonder young adults hesitate to make a commitment to marriage?

To keep a marriage alive and vibrant, couples must spend time together—alone. The emotional, physical, and sexual needs of both parties should be acknowledged. Solutions to the dilemma of "getting away" need to be explored. Budget constraints may prevent an extravagant getaway, but look for alternative ideas. If extended family does not live close enough to allow a couple to have an "alone night" every couple of months, look for friends or acquaintances who are suffering from the same needs. Perhaps you can find a family whose children are similar in age to your children, then swap kids occasionally for an "overnight." Children usually love sleepovers. It's party time.

Although hotels are terrific, being "home alone" can be rejuvenating if you treat home like a hotel. Do not answer the phone; let the answering machine pick up messages. Turn the ringer off. Do not start doing household chores; concentrate on each other. Either eat out, bring in takeout, or prepare food in advance. Light candles. Warm up some scented massage oil. Sleep in late the next morning. Be lazy. Relax. Rekindle the flame of romance.

Talk about your dreams for the future. Someday your "nest" will be empty, like ours is now. Where will your relationship be then? What do you want to do in your retirement years? Set some goals for the two of you. Parents' responsibility is to give their children roots, values to hold them secure throughout life, and wings to take off on their own, flying as high as they want to go. Let children know that your retirement plans do not include supporting them forever.

In the more mundane day-to-day world, putting a simple lock on your bedroom door affords a degree of privacy when children are around the house. Just when you think the children are all asleep and the coast is clear for a little romance, one of the children will have a problem and come knocking on the door. I came to believe that our children had a form of radar. At least, they never "caught" us. They did occasionally ask why the door was locked. We replied that sometimes mommies and daddies like time together—alone. They can figure it out when they are older.

At one particular parenting presentation, a young mother shared a solution that worked for her and her husband. They tell the children they are going to their bedroom to "wrap Christmas presents." No matter what time of year it is, the children never question the idea and they do not disturb the parents. The audience went hysterical. A nun in attendance asked me what was so funny about that story!

I would always worry about what the children might be getting into in our absence. One Saturday morning when we tried something similar, our young sons ate an entire large jar of maraschino cherries they found in the refrigerator. They were bored with the snacks I put out for them to eat while they watched cartoons. Someone told me her child, when left to his own devices, dumped a package of dry Jello into their fish tank in an attempt to feed the fish. Kids! Beware! Oh yes, and be sure to relax and enjoy!

Mention might be made at this point about the popularity of the "family bed" concept. There are many arguments on both sides. From my experience, all I can say is that my husband and I never got a good night's sleep when one of the children had a bad dream or felt ill and came into our bed. There is nothing worse than sleep-deprived parents. We tend to be extremely irritable the following day. Not to even mention the lack of physical closeness with a wiggly, thrashing child between you.

If children get into the habit of coming into the parents' bed, breaking the habit can be very difficult. Establishing the fact that each person in the family has a bed in which to sleep and that is where each person is expected to sleep, gives children a firm guideline to follow. The more exceptions parents make, the harder it becomes for children to accept this rule.

Children who require a parent's proximity to fall asleep do not develop the ability to put themselves to sleep. When awakening during the night, they require a parent's presence again in order to fall back to sleep. Parents get into many bedtime power struggles. Who will win? Nobody! Nip it early by being firm and consistent. The American Academy of Pediatrics has produced an entire book about sleep issues, *Guide to Your Child's Sleep: Birth through Adolescence* (see Appendix 1). Pediatricians consider sleep issues that important.

• Parents as Sexuality Educators

Just using the words "sex education" causes parents to tense up. Oh no, is that part of your job as a parent? Yes it is. Although there is a lot of discussion about the effectiveness of sexuality education in schools, research indicates that the most effective programs in preventing premature sexual activity and teen pregnancy are programs in which parents are empowered as primary educators.

Rarely do parents express an enthusiasm to take on this responsibility. If you relinquish your responsibility to others, there is no guarantee that your family values will be part of the educational process. Currently, media are the most prominent and effective sex educators around. How many young children learned about oral sex during the Clinton-Lewinsky debacle?

Current social mores mandate parents to take an active role in educating their children about the marvelous workings of our God-designed human bodies. Only parents can give children the moral values education that needs to accompany the knowledge of how human bodies function, especially in the area of reproduction. Studies indicate that knowing how humans reproduce is a deterrent to teen pregnancy, not a promoter of it. Many teen pregnancies occur from ignorance and folklore.

Why do parents find the subject so difficult to discuss? Why must we use euphemisms for the biologically correct names of genitalia? Parents are so proud when their child learns to recognize eyes, nose, ears, and such, but what do they reply when the child asks about penis, nipple, labia, and vagina?

Perhaps because my husband is a pediatrician, we always used the correct names for body parts. Etched in my mind forever is a day when my mother and I, along with two-year-old Kevin, went out to lunch. As we were waiting for a table, Kevin was "holding himself." My mother asked him if he had to go to the bathroom. He replied, "No, Grandma, my penis itches!" I thought she was going to pass out. Immediately turning to me, she asked where he had learned THAT word!

We need to get over personal fears about using correct terminology when talking about our human bodies. While giving parenting talks on this matter, I sometimes make participants repeat words from flash cards (such as PENIS, VAGINA, LABIA, SCROTUM), telling them to go home and repeat the words in front of a mirror until they can say them without flinching. A grandmother came up after a talk, giggling. She said that in her whole life she had never said those words out loud!

After sharing these opinions with a friend who had a three-year-old girl and a new baby boy, she shared the following story. She took my advice on using correct names and her daughter seemed comfortable with her brother being different, having a penis. The daughter was assured that she had never had a penis and lost it. This is how God makes men and women different (per my coaching). At Disneyland one day, the mother wanted to clean her daughter's sticky hands, so she got a baby-wipe from the diaper bag. Her daughter announced quite loudly, to everyone nearby, that the wipe was not supposed to be for hands, it was for her brother's penis! My friend said she felt like crawling in a hole. She was embarrassed, but she had done the correct thing. Her daughter is comfortable about differences in human bodies. There is no mystery.

One tip regarding sexuality education is to be sure exactly what question the child is asking. A popular story goes that when a child asked where he came from, his mother got out all the charts and materials she had prepared, ready for this day. After a thorough discussion, the mother asked the child if he had any further questions. His reply was, "Well, Billy said he came from Chicago. Where did I come from?" Clarify the question. Ask: "What do you think the answer is?"

If you are uncomfortable or feel inadequate discussing sexuality, get a good reference book and read up on the subject. Answer children's questions simply, honestly, and promptly. Do not be evasive. If children come to you with questions for which you do not have an answer, agree to find the answer for them. My personal favorite resources come from Concordia Publishing. Their materials, books, and videos contain God-messages throughout. These materials make sex education a religious experience. Everything is according to God's plan. Blame it on God.

"Learning About Sex: A Series for the Christian Family" (see Appendix 1) divides the materials by age groupings: 3 to 5 years, 6 to 8 years, 8 to 11 years, 11 to 14 years, and 14 and up. *Human Sexuality: A Christian Perspective,* also from Concordia, gives a complete, faith-filled, adult examination of sexual issues, in easy-to-understand language. Following a parish presentation on sexuality, during which I showed the video segment "How You Are Changing," for ages 8 to 11, the parish priest who sat in on the talk thanked me, saying he learned quite a bit that evening. Parents and children are not the only ones requiring additional education.

Educate yourselves so that you can talk intelligently with your children about these matters. When you hear a song's lyrics or see a media scene you dislike, use it as a springboard for discussion. Do not be afraid to state your feelings and beliefs. If you do not, who will? Remember that our human bodies are made by God. Sexuality is sacred and needs to be treated respectfully.

Discussion Questions

1. Looking back to your childhood, what affectionate behaviors did you learn from your parents?

2. What is the most embarrassing sexual question one of your children has asked? How did you respond?

3. Out of this past week, seven days, one hundred sixty-eight hours, how much time have you and your spouse devoted exclusively to one another? Where could you make more time for nurturing intimacy?

Chapter 15

Morality

Proverbs 28:5–6—
"The evil do not understand justice, / but those who
seek the LORD / understand it completely. / Better to be
poor and walk in integrity / than to be crooked in one's
/ ways even though rich."

• Role Models of Values

How many times have you heard, "Do as I say, not as I do!"?
Especially in parenting, this does not work. Children, ever watchful of their parents' actions, mirror back to us many of our shortcomings. While grocery shopping one day with my preschooler,
he responded to my nagging by placing his hands on his hips,
looking me in the eye, and saying, with perfect inflection, "YOU
are giving ME a headache!" Wherever did he hear that?

Therefore, if we want to transmit strong moral values to our
children, our lives must exemplify our beliefs. Honesty, as was
discussed in Chapter 1, remains a foundational building block,
being intimately linked to trust in one another. Two other key
components are integrity and reliability.

Integrity involves knowing right from wrong, and choosing
to do the right thing. Making decisions and good choices takes a
lifetime of practice. Start working with children when they are

young. Give children opportunities to make choices, weighing all options. Let them live with the results of their choice; it is the only way they can learn for themselves.

Sometimes it is hard to watch them make wrong choices, and just stand by ready to pick up the pieces. Give them another opportunity later to make another decision. Hopefully, the next time their choice will be better. You do not need to constantly remind them of previous bad decisions and consequences. They remember, even more than they let on to you.

Reliability involves relationships with others. Can you be counted on? Do you keep your word? When you say you will do something, do you follow through? Children need to be able to count on parents to keep their word and be reliable, if they are to emulate that quality. Stress with children the importance of being dependable; it will get them ahead in life. Show them how.

Punctuality is a form of reliability since it ties in with keeping your word. Although there are many far worse faults than being late, developing that habit becomes irritating to others. Try to instill in your children a respect for other people's time by being punctual. People joke about the Anglo culture being too stressed out about being on time. Some people get more irritated than others about tardiness. Those who are hypercritical have probably not raised a houseful of children. Things happen. Plan for the unexpected. Allow extra time. We used to joke about my mother taking her purse and getting in the car a half hour before we needed to leave. Now, when the family's together, I find myself repeating similar behavior, but I no longer run around making sure everyone has a jacket, hair combed, shoes on, and "gone potty."

• Development of Conscience

Knowing right from wrong is not a skill children develop automatically, like walking. Careful schooling is needed in the development of a "right conscience." Basic moral values flow from the Ten Commandments, God's guidelines for a good, productive, and happy life. Parents need to take an adult look at these principles and see what profound messages God is giving us.

Christian parents must carry moral training a step further by incorporating the teachings of Jesus as found in the New Testament. Since mankind did not seem to learn the lessons of the Old Testament, Christ became human to show us the way, the truth, and the light. By his death we are redeemed. Our gratitude should be overwhelming. How do we express our gratefulness to God in our everyday lives?

A few years ago a Christian movement started among youth. WWJD (What Would Jesus Do?) became a popular slogan. WWJD can be found on tee shirts, banners, posters, and jewelry. I found it very heartening when Catholic youth groups joined the crusade with other denominations. All people need to work together to help children find the right paths through the minefield of today's world.

Catholic parents have an additional responsibility to instruct their children in the moral principles set forth by the church. Sending children to parochial school or religious education does not exempt parents from personal responsibility. Sometimes eighth grade was the last time parents received any religious formation. If that is the case, perhaps it is time to update yourself on matters of faith and morals.

Many Catholic periodicals are available. A wealth of books on spirituality and church doctrine may be purchased at Catholic bookstores, or over the Internet (see Appendix 2). Attend talks given in your area; check your parish bulletin or contact your diocesan office for information. We cannot expect more enthusiasm for God from our children than we exhibit in our own lives.

Some older Catholics harbor grudges against the church for early training that may have resulted in overly scrupulous consciences. Mortal and venial sin, guilt, and punishment were guiding principles. Now some of us can look back and laugh, even make jokes about rules and regulations. "Catholic humor" is often based on making fun of those "old days."

When our daughter was attending Catholic high school, she told us one night at dinner that her religion project was to discuss the concept of sin. I asked what was currently being taught on that subject, since things had changed so much since I was in Catholic high school. The discussion that ensued forced me to dig out a cartoon joke book entitled *You've Survived Catholic School When...!* (out of print), which had been a gift. These were the so-called sins of my youth.

Kristy found them so unbelievable that she made overheads of some cartoons to illustrate her oral presentation. The subject of her report was: How can parents and children discuss moral issues when they are coming at the subject from such diverse positions? Her instructor, a priest, was so impressed that she received an A+++. The students found extraordinary the ideas of no sleeveless dresses, no pullover sweaters without a blouse underneath, no patent leather shoes, no dancing closer than two telephone books, the belief that reading *National Geographic* could be an occasion of sin, and so on.

"Let your conscience be your guide" only works when a person has received training in forming a right conscience. Humanism, secularism, and hedonism exert far greater pressure in American society today than fundamental Christian principles of putting God first in your life, loving your neighbor as yourself, and doing unto others as you would have them do unto you.

Public schools will not, or administrators say they cannot, assume the task of teaching moral values. The argument is, whose moral values would schools teach? Could agreement ever be reached to satisfy all Americans? Our society is based on the rights of the individual, not the good of society as a whole. Therefore, the responsibility of teaching strong moral values falls upon parents, ready or not!

Instruction in moral development means taking positions that children may fight against. The old "but everybody else is..." remains a popular refrain. I would hear myself echoing my mother's words: "If everybody else jumped off a bridge, would you?" Some things never change.

As I indicated previously, our children would get aggravated with our moralizing during television programs. We did not allow MTV to be on if we were not around to supervise. Often, upon returning home, we would hear them quickly change stations; they knew our values. The same quick changing of radio stations would occur if the children knew an upcoming song meant a lecture from Mom.

When cable television was brought into our area we refused the movie channels, not wanting to allow influences into our home with which we did not agree. A neighbor said I was fooling myself if I thought my children were not going to neighbors' homes and watching "those" movies. My reply was that at least they would be feeling guilty, and that might spoil some of the fun! Parents can only do so much. But do give children the benefit of guidance or they will have no moral compass.

• Respect for Others

The rights of the individual over the good of society in general has become the battle cry of American society. Freedom of speech has been carried to extremes never dreamt of by this country's founding fathers. The right to bear arms, hotly debated by so many, contributes daily to the death toll from violence. Drug usage has become so commonplace that burglary, theft, and assault occur in every city, every day, and at every economic level to support drug dependencies. Respect for other people and their property rights is eroding.

Teaching children to respect the rights of other people must start young. Research shows that children as young as eighteen months of age can have empathy for others. This ability to recognize another as sad or hurt must be nurtured. Talking about how actions affect others is essential if parents are to make an impact.

Demonstrating concern for the welfare of others should be extended to the community by becoming involved in charitable endeavors. Collecting used clothing, toys, books, and food to be taken to homeless shelters, homes for battered women, or other charitable institutions becomes most effective when the children are involved in selecting items to be given and helping to deliver the items. Look for volunteer opportunities that are available all year long. My young nephew asked his mother if there were poor people in Los Angeles. There are.

Respect needs to be shown in words, also. Talk in the home should be free of crudity, bigotry, and blasphemy. Blasphemy sounds very old-fashioned, but taking God's name in vain should not be a joking matter. It behooves parents to clean up their language and not allow anyone in the home to use disrespectful language. Even though I grew up with two brothers, I never heard any bad language in our home. My mother did not allow it. As simple as that. My husband and I have always tried to keep our home free of crudity, reminding the children of this if something "slipped out." In return, they always remind us if we slip.

Ethnic slurs and jokes teach disrespect, and can be hurtful. Our family heritage is Polish, so we know firsthand how hurtful Polish jokes can be. My daughter, a natural blonde, really detests "blonde jokes." Discuss with children the value of all human beings as part of God's family. Examine the likenesses, as well as the differences, among human beings. An early childhood instructor told us not to be afraid to cut up old *National Geographic* magazines, as they are not sacred, and using them to make posters showing similarities between people of different races and cultures: children with their parents; families eating, playing, working together; people laughing, crying, praying. Human beings have so many similarities. God loves all of us—unconditionally—and asks us to love one another in the same way.

Any form of abuse reduces our humanity. Emotional abuse can take the simple form of teasing, belittling, or shaming. Making fun of people, causing them emotional and psychological distress, is abuse. Verbal abuse stems not only from the words spoken to others, but includes tone of voice. Many parents do not recognize chronic screaming at children as a form of child abuse. It is.

Sexual abuse of children in physical forms is always abhorrent, but consider if forms of pornography do get into your home. Are young children exposed to inappropriate sexual media? MTV? Is there sufficient supervision of cable television channels, as well as the commercial channels? What magazines come into the home? What type of music is played? What do the lyrics say?

Alcohol and drug abuse, two common family problems, should not be tolerated. If either is affecting your family, seek help. The effects on children are devastating, and very long lasting.

Kids are people too! Treat them with respect!

Discussion Questions

1. Describe the most reliable person you know. What qualities about that person sets him or her apart from others?

2. Many people imagine conscience as a good angel on one shoulder, and a bad angel on the other shoulder, both fighting for attention. How would you explain the concept of "conscience" to your children? How do you tell right from wrong?

3. Looking back to your childhood, list any of your parents' actions that might now be considered a form of child abuse—such as frequent spankings. Try to remember how you, as a child, felt about the behavior. Write it down. Burn the paper, letting go of any hurt. Forgive them for shortcomings. We are all just human.

Chapter 16

Evaluation

Proverbs 19:20—
"Listen to advice and accept instruction, / that you may
gain wisdom for the future."

• Review Family Life

How are things going in your family? After reading this
book, do you see areas where improvement can be made? Have
you congratulated yourself on all the good things you are already
doing? Be proud of the strong, positive points. Compare your
family with other families in your acquaintance. Are there things
you can learn from their strengths, and weaknesses?

In 1984, my husband's cousin and her family came from
Minnesota for a California vacation with us. After returning
home, she sent me a wonderful letter of gratitude. What she was
most grateful for was the example my husband provided to her
husband of affectionate, physical contact with our children. Her
husband had grown up in an undemonstrative Germanic family.
He was never hugged. He found it difficult to hug his children,
especially when they were no longer toddlers. After two weeks of
interacting with us, he made a commitment to change his ways.
His wife said it was wonderful to watch the change in relationship
between him and his children.

Touch is one of the most basic human needs. Children in orphanages have been shown to die from lack of touch, even though they were fed, bathed, and basically cared for. Cuddling and hugging creates a bond with children, helps them thrive, not merely survive. Child psychologists say children need to be lovingly touched fifty times a day for good mental health. Everyone needs to be touched and affirmed. Remember to include adults with a pat on the back or other gesture of affection.

When my husband finished medical training, we looked at the families of several doctors we knew. We could tell that doctors in private practice had limited time to be with their families due to the pace of medical practice. We made a conscious decision for him to join a group practice where, although the monetary rewards might not be as large, time with family would be available. Lon has never regretted his decision. He has been involved in YMCA Indian Guides/Princesses, Boy Scouts, youth ministry, Sunday school, camping, fishing, hiking, biking, and numerous other activities with the family throughout the years. Our family bonds are stronger for his efforts. For my part, I chose to be a full-time homemaker to better meet the needs of my family. Material goods have never been as important to us as spending time together. I realize, however that being a full-time homemaker is sometimes not an option.

• Use Educational Resources

Check the magazines at the market check-out stands. There is a plethora of parent educational material available. Read articles. Pick up books, especially ones recommended by friends, and READ them. Do not just put the books on a shelf. Having resources in the house does not put information in your brain by osmosis. The public library is a treasure-house of resources and librarians are always ready to help. Most libraries have video sections, in addition to books and magazines. Take young children to Story Hour, then you can browse. Think about how much study goes into career development. Parenting is the most important career in the world.

Watch educational programs on parenting. Check the television listings, particularly Public Television stations. If an informative program comes on at an inconvenient time, use your video recorder. Watch the program when the time is convenient and you and your spouse can watch together. Build a library of programs, loaning them to friends, or start a parenting library at your parish. Be a support group for one another.

The Internet is filled with resources, if you make time to browse. Magazines and newspapers often print lists of educational web sites. Keep a list of their addresses.

• Seek Professional Help

After reviewing the material in this book, if you feel your family life is out of control do not hesitate to seek professional help. When problems have gone beyond your ability to solve or deal with them, get an outside opinion. If you feel that you are reaching the limit of your endurance, take action before something unfortunate happens.

A *Good Housekeeping* magazine article described a care center in New York City, the NYC Crisis Nursery, that helps parents who feel unable to cope with their children. The center accepts children for an overnight stay, then provides parents with parent education to improve their skills in handling the responsibilities of parenting. Sometimes, the article stated, all parents needed was a break in the tension, and a few good alternative ideas for handling discipline. If necessary, the center can put parents in touch with ongoing help.[16] Wouldn't it be wonderful if every community, especially faith communities, provided such a compassionate solution for parenting stress?

Discussion Questions

1. On a scale of one to ten, ten being "the perfect family" and one being "disaster zone," have all of your family members rank your family. Ask them to explain their answers. Discuss.

2. Get the current television guide. Review the week, looking for parent education programs. Pick out one and watch it with your spouse. Discuss.

3. Pressures in today's world are far different from fifty years ago. Does a stigma of seeing a therapist exist in your mind? Describe any experience you or a family member has had with therapy. Was the result positive or negative? How does this affect your opinion?

Section 5

Resources/Appendices

Appendix 1

※

Resources Cited in Text

American Academy of Pediatrics, publisher
    (www.aap.org, or phone 888-227-1770)
    Caring for Your Baby and Young Child: Birth to Age 5
    [ISBN:0553071866]
    Steven P. Shelov, M.D., F.A.A.P., Editor-in-chief
    Caring for Your School-Age Child: Ages 5 to 12 [ISBN:0553099817]
    Edward L. Schor, M.D., F.A.A.P., Editor-in-chief
    Caring for Your Adolescent: Ages 12 to 21 [ISBN:055307556X]
    Donald E. Greydanus, M.D., F.A.A.P., Editor-in-chief
    Guide to Your Child's Nutrition: Making Peace at the Table and
      Building Healthy Eating Habits for Life [ISBN:0375501878]
    William H. Dietz, M.D., F.A.A.P. and Lorraine Stern, M.D.,
    F.A.A.P., Editors
    Guide to Your Child's Sleep: Birth through Adolescence
    [ISBN:0679769811]
    George J. Cohen, M.D., F.A.A.P., Editor-in-chief
American Guidance Service, publisher
    (www.parentingeducation.com, or phone 800-328-2560)
    Systematic Training for Effective Parenting (STEP)
    Authors—Don Dinkmeyer, Sr., Gary D. McKay,
    D. Dinkmeyer, Jr., James Dinkmeyer, Joyce L. McKay
    Parenting Young Children [ISBN:0785411895] (STEP of Children
    Under Six)

Building a Family

The Parent's Handbook [ISBN:0785411887] (STEP of all children)

Parenting Teenagers [ISBN:0886714044] (STEP of Teens)

Brite Music Inc.—Music and lyrics by Janeen Brady, publisher

(www.britemusic.com, or phone 800-264-0693)

Standin' Tall Series—story cassettes/CDs with booklets

(includes Obedience, Honesty, Forgiveness, Work, Courage, Happiness, Gratitude, Love, Service, Cleanliness, Self-Esteem, and Dependability)

Children: The Challenge

Authors—Rudolf Dreikurs, M.D. with Vicki Soltz, R.N. [ISBN:052548308X]

Eight Ways of Knowing: Teaching for Multiple Intelligences

Author—David G. Lazear [ISBN:0932935184]

Learning About Sex: A Series for the Christian Family—

Concordia Publishing

(800-325-3040)

Why Boys and Girls Are Different (Ages 3 to 5)

Author—Carol Greene [ISBN:057003552X]

Where Do Babies Come From? (Ages 6 to 8)

Author—Ruth Hummel [ISBN:0570035538]

How You Are Changing (Ages 8 to 11)

Author—Jane Graver [ISBN:0570035546]

Sex and the New You (Ages 11 to 14)

Author—Richard Bimler [ISBN:0570035554]

Love, Sex, and God (Ages 14 to Adult)

Authors—Bill Ameiss and Jane Graver [ISBN:0570035562]

How to Talk Confidently with Your Child About Sex...and Appreciate Your Own Sexuality Too

Author—Lenore Buth [ISBN:0570035511]

Human Sexuality: A Christian Perspective

Author—Roger Sonnenberg, M.Div [ISBN:0-570-03568-6]

Appendix 1

*Let's Make A Memory: Great Ideas for Building Family Traditions and
Togetherness*
Authors—Gloria Gaither and Shirley Dobson
[ISBN:0849935172]

Life in the Family Zoo
Author—John M. Platt, Ed.D. [ISBN:0962444618]

*Money Doesn't Grow on Trees: A Parent's Guide to Raising Financially
Responsible Children*
Authors—Neale S. Godfrey and Carolina Edwards
[ISBN:0671798057]

The New Birth Order Book: Why You Are the Way You Are
Author—Kevin Leman [ISBN:0800756797]

On Parenting
Author—James C. Dobson, Ph.D. [ISBN:0884861775]

*A Penny Saved: Teaching Your Children the Values and Life Skills They
Will Need to Live in the Real World*
Authors—Neale S. Godfrey and Tad Richards
[ISBN:0684824809]

Please Understand Me: Character and Temperament Types
Authors—David Keirsey and Marilyn Bates
[ISBN:0960695400]

*The Road Less Traveled: A New Psychology of Love, Traditional Values,
and Spiritual Growth*
Author—M. Scott Peck, M.D. [ISBN:0684847248]

*The Search for Common Ground: What Unites and Divides Catholic
Americans*
Authors—James D. Davidson, Andrea S. Williams, Richard
A. Lamanna, Jan Stenftenagel, Kathleen Maas Weigert,
William J. Whalen, Patricia Wittberg, S.C.
[ISBN:0879739258]

Sex, Love, or Infatuation: How Can I Really Know?
Author—Ray Short [ISBN:0806624604]

Appendix 2

Web Sites for Resources/Catalogs

www.cambridgeeducational.com

> Cambridge Parenting & Family Life—comprehensive resources, books and videos—800-468-4227

www.childfaith.com

> Caring Family Resources—a collection of writings, books, and music to help parents more effectively influence spiritual development and value education—310-325-4118

www.childrensdefense.org

> Children's Defense Fund—a multitude of resources for raising awareness among Americans of the need to concentrate effort on the plight of our nation's children—202-662-3652

www.familytv.com

> Feature Films for Families—inexpensive videos specifically selected for family viewing and value education—800-326-4598

www.ignatius.com

> Ignatius Press—an extensive list of religious videos available—800-651-1531

www.medialit.org

> Center for Media Literacy—resources to help families learn to be discriminating television viewers—800-226-9494

www.nccbuscc.org

> National Conference of Catholic Bishops/United States Catholic Conference—listings of all papal, Vatican, and bishops' documents, plus an extensive collection of Catholic resource books/videos—800-235-8722

www.parenting.org

> Fr. Flanagan's Boys' Home-sponsored Common Sense Parenting Newsletter, books and videos—800-498-4900

www.parentingeducation.com

> American Guidance Service—many resources that would help build a great parish parenting library—800-328-2560

www.saxusa.com

> Sax Life Skills Resources—terrific resources for parish, school, and parenting libraries—800-558-6696

www.SimpleLiving.org

> Alternatives for Simple Living—programs, books, and videos to help people live more simply and practice Christian peace and justice, plus some wonderful Advent and Lent resources—800-821-6153

There are lots more parenting resources available on "The Net"!

Appendix 3

Suggestions for Parent Education

• Why is the nurturing of families important?

In a society as fast-paced as today's has become, families are stressed to the limit. There never seems to be enough time to get everything accomplished. Work demands conflict with educational needs, fitness goals, recreational activities, hobbies, church involvement, volunteerism, family time, and effective parenting.

Parents often say they need help, but when can they fit in a series of classes, a workshop, or even the reading of a book? Is there a way the church can help? Yes, the church is in a key position to offer assistance with an emphasis on the family perspective. Let parents know that both the church and God care deeply about their succeeding in the important and challenging task God has bestowed on them.

In yesteryear, extended families lived in close proximity and passed on values, skills, and knowledge. Large families meant that children learned about caring for siblings, sharing, having work responsibilities, and living in a cooperative environment. Nowadays families are smaller, many children have no siblings, or perhaps only one. Single parent families abound. Many children do not experience caring for siblings, sharing rooms, toys, clothes, or having work responsibilities around the house.

While attending a baby shower recently for a friend's daughter, I was astounded to hear that the mother-to-be has never changed a diaper. There is much knowledge that new parents, and parents of young children, could learn from mentor parents who have survived the parenting process. The church has the opportunity for such interaction, especially during the prebaptismal period when parents are asking to have their child welcomed into the faith community.

Wouldn't it be wonderful to have an experienced couple volunteer to mentor one couple through the perilous first years? Just to have someone to call for reassurance, a listening ear, a helping hand, a caring heart. Although the saying has become somewhat hackneyed, it does "take a village to raise a child." We all have to care and accept some responsibility for the nurturing of families if we want to see an improvement in society.

Another opportunity for enhancing parenting skills that can be utilized within the church setting are the obligatory parent meetings held by both parish schools and religious education departments. Allowing some time at these meetings to review parenting skills may whet parents' appetites to learn more. A dynamic fun-type presentation will possibly have them asking for more such meetings.

• Using this book as an outline for parent presentations

Being involved in early childhood catechesis for over twenty years, having been program coordinator on both parish and diocesan levels, and having had experience as a parenting columnist for the diocesan newspaper, I often get called upon to be a speaker. This book is the result of one of my most popular parenting talks, which I developed with the assistance of my husband, a dedicated pediatrician who is also involved in the faith formation of young children. Our hope is that those reading the book will not only gain knowledge for themselves, but also become inspired to share the ideas it contains with others in their parish, school, neighborhood, and family.

A lot of "God-talk" runs throughout the book because we feel strongly about the need to emphasize God's action in everyone's life. When giving the presentation to secular parenting groups, the God-talk can be eliminated. Having worked with school districts in our area, we know there are rules that must be followed.

An effective means of presenting the topics is by obtaining a large presentation board from an office or school supply company, or covering a pattern cutting board from a fabric store with a solid color Contact paper. Print across the top of the board in very large letters T I M E. Then on smaller pieces of paper print out the words found as the headings for each chapter, that is, Trust, Individuality, and so on. Depending on the size of your audience, make the words big enough to be read by everyone, or give them a handout with the words printed on it so they can take notes as you speak.

The words give you focus and an outline to follow as you give your presentation. This both keeps you organized, and impresses the audience that you do not need to read the talk from notes. Following an introduction, put the first word up under "T" and discuss that subject, then proceed to the "I" word, and so on. I use Velcro strips to hold the words, or the sticky substance called "Fun Tack," which is used to put up papers and decorations.

If you only have one opportunity to speak to a group of parents, you can go briefly over each of the sixteen topics, but it hits parents with a lot of information in a very short time. I usually warn parents not to try and take notes on everything. "Concentrate on ideas you have not heard before or areas where your particular family needs improvement. Congratulate yourselves on all the things you are already doing well!"

A better plan would be to meet four times and have time for group discussion and interaction. Covering only one section of the book at a session provides plenty of material. Parents have terrific, creative ideas to share with one another given the opportunity and encouragement. Gatherings such as this help to build a sense of community and can be the springboard for friendships, play groups, babysitting exchanges, and parent clubs. In other words—Fellowship!

Handouts and lists of resources can be provided to partici-pants. Some suggestions are included in Section 5. *My* personal stories are included in this book, but I would encourage each of you to develop *your* stories, making the talk your own. We are all journeying together but our paths are very different. Sharing the story of our journey is what being a Christian is all about.

Appendix 4

Parenting Handouts

(Handouts created from a variety of resources collected over the years. Definitive sources not available.)

Parenting Prayer
by Marilyn Spaw Krock

Lord, we come before you today with deep concern for the children of today's world. Believing sincerely in your promise that wherever two or more are gathered in your name, you are here in our midst, we ask you to touch our hearts and minds that we might think, act, and love as you desire. By striving to be your hands and voice in the world, help us to build up your kingdom of love on earth.

As we pray in fellowship, we lift up the needs of each of us in our various roles of parenting and caregiving. We recall the African proverb, "It takes a village to raise a child." Raising a child is so much more than just being a parent! Webster's dictionary definitions bear this out! TO PARENT: to bring forth, bear, beget. TO RAISE: to rear and bring up; to cause to grow; to bring from a lower place to a higher; to lift up; to enhance; to increase in size and value; to increase the intensity, strength, and power; to excite; to rouse to action; to awaken.

Help us, dear God, to see the many ways each of us can touch the lives of children in our families, neighborhoods, country, and world. Help us to recognize the needs of children at each stage of their development. We know that the way children grow and blossom is part of your divine plan, just as the other miracles of nature are signs of your infinite love for us.

WE LIFT UP THE NEEDS OF THOSE RAISING CHILDREN IN THE EARLY YEARS

These years are crucial to healthy development. Help children develop trust in people through their needs being consistently and lovingly met. When children learn to trust parents and early caregivers, they learn to trust others. When we learn to trust others, we can learn to trust in you, God. Being concrete thinkers, children come to a knowledge of you through their relationships with us. Remind us constantly that we are "God-with-skin-on" to young children. The image they are forming of you is in our hands! Help us learn to make time to be with young children, sharing the wonder of your magnificent creation, thus inspiring in them a sense of gratitude to you for your many gifts.

WE LIFT UP THE NEEDS OF THOSE RAISING CHILDREN IN THE MIDDLE YEARS

As we send these children forth into the world of school and society, help us to send them forth with a strong foundation that can withstand the buffeting of life. Help us give them a strong sense of self-esteem, knowing that you made them for a purpose; they are important; they are unique, unrepeatable images of your love. Help us to teach them values, so that they may not be swayed by forces contrary to our beliefs. As we teach and guide our children, Lord, keep us mindful that the root of the word *discipline* comes from the Latin word meaning "to train." Let us allow them, Lord, to make choices, learning from their mistakes, and accepting responsibility for the consequences, for that is how children learn; it is your plan!

WE LIFT UP THE NEEDS OF THOSE RAISING CHILDREN IN THE TEENAGE YEARS

As our children struggle for independence and the autonomy of becoming their own persons, help us Lord to remember what those tumultuous years were like for us. Let us learn to be good listeners, helping them work through their problems by being there when they need us, not with answers, but with compassion. Help us be reasonable in our expectations and forgiving as you are forgiving, Lord, always ready to reconcile. Let us model to our teens the respect, kindness, and patience we hope to receive from them, so that they might see a reflection of your unconditional love in us. Give us strength to stand up for our beliefs and values, letting teens know what we believe in and why, ever mindful that what we do speaks louder than what we say.

WE LIFT UP THE NEEDS OF THOSE RAISING CHILDREN IN THE YOUNG ADULT YEARS

As we are called to release our adult children into the world, give us confidence that we have done well during their formative years. Help us to let go of our role as "parent" and form a new relationship, "adult to adult." Make us worthy of their friendship, treating them as we would treat a good friend. Lord, we have tried to give them roots; help us encourage them to use their wings. Guide them to form healthy relationships with others. Help us to be accepting of these relationships, trusting their judgment, letting them assume responsibility for their actions, and accepting the consequences of their choices. Remind us again Lord to trust you to take care of them; our job as parent ends, but our love for them is eternal, and in that love there is sometimes pain. Heal any wounds. Strengthen the family bonds of love for of such is the Kingdom of God!

WE LIFT UP THE NEEDS OF SINGLE PARENTS

Lord, raising children is a difficult calling. Give added strength to those who are journeying this path alone; give them comfort and solace in times of loneliness. Help all of us to be watchful for opportunities to reach out and lighten the load of these parents with an encouraging word, a small act of kindness, or special prayers. Inspire us, Lord, to assist children in these families by giving our time to be with them through various programs in our churches and in our community.

Let these families see our faith in action as we form a community of love and support.

WE LIFT UP THE NEEDS OF GRANDPARENTS

Let us find joy in the gift of grandchildren, the continuance of our heritage, our link with immortality. Special blessings, we ask Lord, for those grandparents called on to raise their grandchildren, either part time or full time, due to circumstances in today's world. Help them to turn to you with their needs. Give them extra patience and love to meet the sometimes overwhelming demands of growing children. Help them to be open to new ideas, while holding on to old-fashioned values. Let them learn to trust in you for guidance and strength.

WE LIFT UP THE NEEDS OF THOSE CARING FOR ILL OR AGING PARENTS

As our parents' journey through this earthly life nears completion, Lord, help us to remember the good times we have shared, and the joys we have known in their loving care. Strengthen us and increase our patience with them as they struggle with the concept of dependence. Remind us, Lord, of how we treasure our independence throughout life and the ability to take care of ourselves and make our own decisions. Make us more understanding of the losses they are suffering. Let us love them with the unconditional love that we have learned from you, Lord. Then when the time comes to let go of our parents, allowing them return to you, we will find peace in knowing we have loved each other well as we journeyed together in this life.

WE KNOW WE ARE ASKING A LOT LORD, BUT WE TRUST THAT IN YOU ALL THINGS ARE POSSIBLE, ESPECIALLY WHEN WE ASK THEM IN JESUS' NAME. AMEN.

Appendix 4

Tips for Making Time

Come home from work and change clothes first.

Use the answering machine. Don't interrupt family time.

Let children know that if they all do their tasks quickly, there will be time to play together.

Plan quick and easy meals ahead of time. Get children involved in preparing dinner with you. After dinner everyone helps clean up.

Then take time to play a game, read a story, or give a back rub.

Designate one child each night to be "special"—he or she picks game or book.

Try to avoid arguing or nagging.

Children want your attention—negative attention is as good as positive.

Remember, behavior that is rewarded (with your TIME) will repeat itself.

Read to your child each night; try one chapter of a classic.

Before sleep, spend some time with each child reflecting on the day and praying together.

Get children to bed early enough that you have adult time.

If the TV is off after dinner, children can be BORED to bed.

Ration TV/screen time! Television/computer games/Internet are the most significant time drains.

Do not over-schedule your children with activities (sports, music).

On weekends combine chores with family time.

Schedule fun time along with errands—a park, beach, movie, snack.

Surprise the family with a "mental health day"; play hooky together.

Be organized. Put all schedules onto a master calendar. Keep it convenient. Make it large!

Be sure to have all family members put all of their activities on the calendar.

Set priorities! Adjust expectations!

"Our home is clean enough to be healthy, dirty enough to be happy."
Ask for help. Family members aren't mind readers.
Tell them how they can assist in household tasks.
Try to leave your "work" at work, so that your family has your full
     attention when you are home. If necessary, work after the chil-
     dren are in bed, but you may be shortchanging your spouse.

Keeping Your Child's Self-Image Strong

Say something positive to your child each day.

Try to see that your child achieves success in some way each day by offering a variety of activities.

Give your child recognition for the effort she makes even though it may not be up to your expectations.

Make your child feel he belongs.

Listen to your child and look her in the eye when she is talking.

Touch your child lovingly and OFTEN each day.

Answer your child's questions openly, honestly, and immediately, if possible.

Do not embarrass your child, especially in front of others.

Do not make him question his worth.

Compliment the child when possible on creative ideas, improvements, and so forth.

Encourage your child to be proud of her name, work, ideas.

Do not set goals so high that the chance of failure prevents your child from trying.

Emphasize what your child does right instead of what he does wrong.

Treat your child as you would like to be treated, or as well as you treat your friends.

Shaming a Child

Shame is one frequently used weapon in parents' arsenal of discipline strategies. The big gun we pull out when we've reached the end of our rope. Put-down remarks assault the child's sense of self-worth and are humiliating.

Shame *vs.* Guilt

Guilt is when you feel bad about something you have done.

Shame is when you feel bad about who you are.

Shaming statements make the child feel worthless or inadequate rather than being directed at the offending behavior.

- Shame is in our cultural roots: "You should be ashamed of yourself." We often react as our parents treated us.

- Parents often project their own sense of shame onto the child for traits they cannot tolerate in themselves.

- Teasing can easily become shaming when it involves ridicule or belittling.

Consequences of Shaming

- Long-standing psychological damage.

- Backfires by creating anger and hostility in the child.

- Doesn't inform the child about what the problem is or how to solve it.

- Can reinforce the behavior the parent wants to change because the child becomes discouraged and feels incapable of better behavior.

- Damages parent-child relationship.

Better Ways to Discipline

- Have reasonable expectations—learn child development.

- Use encouragement to boost child's self-confidence.

- Criticize behavior, not the child.

- Don't be afraid to apologize when you realize you erred.

Appendix 4

Getting Along with Others

Keep skid chains on your tongue; always say less than you think.

Cultivate a slow, persuasive voice.

How you say it often counts for more than what you say.

Make promises sparingly and keep them faithfully, no matter what it costs.

Never let an opportunity pass to say a kind and encouraging thing to or about somebody.

Praise good work done, regardless of who did it.

If criticism is merited, criticize helpfully, never spitefully or sarcastically.

Be interested in others—their pursuits, their welfare, their homes and families.

Make merry with those who rejoice, and mourn with those who weep.

Let all those you meet, however humble, feel that you regard them as persons of importance.

Be cheerful. Keep the corners of your mouth turned up.

Hide your pain, worries, and disappointments under a pleasant smile.

Laugh at good stories and learn to tell them.

Preserve an open mind on all debatable questions. Discuss, but don't argue.

It is a mark of superior minds to disagree and yet be friendly.

Let your virtues speak for themselves, and refuse to talk of another's vices.

Discourage gossip, and make it a good rule to say nothing of another unless it is something good.

Be careful of others' feelings.

Wit and humor at another's expense is rarely worth the effort, and may hurt where least expected.

Pay no attention to ill-natured remarks about you. Simply live so
    nobody will believe them.

Don't be too anxious about getting your "just dues."

Do your work, be patient, keep your disposition sweet, forget self,
    and you will be respected and rewarded, if not in this life—
    in the next!

Appendix 4

Seven Steps to Maturity

Gaining self-control is the cornerstone of maturity. Self-control is defined as "restraint exercised over one's own impulses, emotions, or desires." It involves learning the following skills:

Step 1—Accepting Responsibility

- learning standards they are expected to live up to, limits they must observe, and responsibilities to be fulfilled

- children must face consequences of their behavior

Step 2—Sticking to a Schedule

- parents can help by blocking out, in writing, hours for specific obligations

- limit television viewing—no TV in bedroom

Step 3—Listening to Directions

- play "statue"—have child sit still for as long as possible without moving, work on increasing the time

- have child follow silly commands, like "Simon Says"

- have child repeat instructions you give to him or her

Step 4—Abiding by the Rules

- merge "school rules" with "home rules" for continuity in learning a sense of order and respect for rules

- make consequences for breaking rules known in advance

- enforce consequences consistently

Step 5—Taming Angry Feelings

- teach child a TO DO not a DON'T DO

- take a deep breath and count to ten

- say: "It makes me angry when you do that."

Building a Family

- set a good example—and stay calm and firm

- give attention for good behavior, not misbehavior

Step 6—Patience Takes Practice
- stay with the child while he or she tackles a task

- encourage to reinforce perseverance

- if a child becomes frustrated—teach him or her to cope with the feelings

- role play behaviors and consequences

Step 7—Delaying Gratification
- teach a child to think ahead

- distract from persistent requests, put off satisfaction

- teach the children to save up for what they want

Discussion Questions for Family TV Viewing

What did I gain from watching this show?

Was there something more worthwhile I could have been doing?

What was real about it? What was fantasy?

How did you feel while watching it?

Could the same thing have happened to you?

Is it possible, or is it pretend?

Why do you like the superhero?

What things can he/she do that you cannot do? That you can do?

What sound effects have been added to make the show more exciting?

How do the characters relate to one another?

Do they treat each other with respect?

Are the problems they face real in YOUR life?

What activities do the characters do together?

Do children interact with parents?

Do they talk about their feelings?

Do characters fight and then make up?

Which characters would you want for a friend? Why?

Are there any older people on the show? What are they doing?

Do you see any handicapped people? How are they portrayed?

Could a handicapped person play the lead role in your favorite show?

How would that change the show?

Are commercials making promises they can't keep?

What do you remember about the ad? Music? Jingle? Characters?

Would you have wanted this product if you had not seen the commercial?

Does the product look like that in real life?

Dos and Don'ts of Sex Education

DON'T feel that your child is too young to have a particular question about sexuality answered. If that were true, the child would not have asked the question in the first place.

DO teach your children the CORRECT terms for the parts of the body associated with reproduction and elimination, just as you teach them the proper names for other bodily parts and functions.

DON'T assume that because your children do not ask questions about sexual matters, they are not curious. If they do not ask questions by the time they are five or six years old, bring up the subject.

When your child asks a question, DO give short, simple answers. If the child wants to know more, he or she will let you know. Remember, it's easier to add information than take it away.

DON'T put off answering questions. To a young child, "later" or "another time" means NEVER. The child may not ask again.

DO try to find out how much the child already knows or thinks he/she knows about the subject under discussion before giving information. Use the "What do you think?" technique.

DO let your children know they can talk to you about any subject, including sexuality, and that if you do not know the answer to the question, you will help them find out the answer.

If you give the child a book (or video) explaining reproduction and childbirth, DO read it with the child so you can answer questions and clear up any misunderstandings.

More important than what you tell your children about sexuality, or when you talk to them, is HOW you talk to them. Whenever you are talking to your child about the facts of human reproduction and sexuality, try to remember to use the word LOVE.

151

As Christians, DO get comfortable bringing God into the subject of sexuality. God made us male and female. Sexuality is part of God's plan for the continuation of the human species.

We are more highly developed than animals. We have intellect and free will. Learning to use our God-given gift of sexuality according to God's plan is religious education!

Notes

1. Steven P. Shelov, Editor-in-chief, *Caring for Your Baby and Young Child* (New York: Bantam Books, 1993), p. xx.

2. Janeen Brady, *Standin' Tall with Honesty* (Brite Music Enterprises, Inc., 1982).

3. Don Dinkmeyer and Gary D. McKay, *Parenting Teenagers: Systematic Training for Effective Parenting of Teens* (Circle Pines, Minn.: American Guidance Service, 1990), pp. 6–7.

4. David Keirsey and Marilyn Bates, *Please Understand Me* (Del Mar Calif.: Prometheus Nemesis Book Co., 1984), pp. 14–16.

5. David Lazear, *Eight Ways of Knowing: Teaching for Multiple Intelligences* (Arlington Heights, Ill.: SkyLight Professional Development, 1999), pp. 1–7.

6. Dr. Kevin Leman, *The New Birth Order Book: Why You Are the Way You Are* (Grand Rapids, Mich.: Fleming H. Revell, 2000).

7. Richard Fowler, Ph.D., "How to Raise a Well Adjusted Parent," presentation given at 1981 Los Angeles Archdiocesan Religious Education Congress.

8. James C. Dobson, Ph.D., *On Parenting* (New York: Inspirational Press, 1997), p. 278.

9. M. Scott Peck, M.D., *The Road Less Traveled* (New York: Simon & Schuster, 1978), p. 230.

10. Neale S. Godfrey, *Money Doesn't Grow on Trees* (New York: Fireside, 1994), pp. 43–44.

11. Neale S. Godfrey, *A Penny Saved* (New York: Fireside, 1995).

12. Hyrum W. Smith, *The Power of Time Control* (The Franklin Institute Time Management Seminar, 1986).

13. Godfrey, *A Penny Saved,* p. 17.

14. John M. Platt, Ed.D., *Life in the Family Zoo* (Roseville, Calif.: Dynamic Training and Seminars, Inc., 1991).

15. Ray Short, *Sex, Love, or Infatuation: How Can I Really Know?* (Minneapolis: Augsburg Publishing House, 1990).

16. Joanna Powell, "Welcome the Little Children," *Good Housekeeping* (January 2001), pp. 66–70

Bibliography

Books on Parenting Skills

Secular

Brazelton, T. Berry. *Infants and Mothers*. New York: Dell Publishing Co., 1983.

_____. *Toddlers and Parents*. New York: Dell Publishing Co., 1974.

Cohen, George J., M.D., Editor-in-chief. *Guide to Your Child's Sleep*. New York; Random House, Inc., 1999.

Davitz, Joel Robert, Ph.D. and Lois Leiderman Davitz, Ph.D. *How to Live (Almost) Happily with a Teenager*. Minneapolis: Winston Press, Inc., 1982.

Dietz, William H., M.D., and Loraine Stern, M.D., Editors. *Guide to Your Child's Nutrition*. New York: Random House, Inc., 1999.

Dinkmeyer, Don, and Gary D. McKay. *Parenting Teenagers*. Circle Pines, Minn.: American Guidance Service, Inc., 1990.

Dinkmeyer, Don, Gary D. McKay, and Don Dinkmeyer, Jr. *The Parent's Handbook*. Circle Pines, Minn.: American Guidance Service, Inc., 1997.

Dinkmeyer, Don, Gary D. McKay, Don Dinkmeyer, Jr., James S. Dinkmeyer, and Joyce L. McKay. *The Effective Parent*. Circle Pines, Minn.: American Guidance Service, Inc., 1987.

Dinkmeyer, Don, Gary D. McKay, Don Dinkmeyer, Jr., James S. Dinkmeyer, and Joyce L. McKay. *Parenting Young Children*. Circle Pines, Minn.: American Guidance Service, Inc., 1997.

Dreikurs, Rudolf, M.D., and Vicki Soltz, R.N. *Children: The Challenge*. New York: E. P. Dutton, 1964.

Elkind, David. *The Hurried Child*. Menlo Park, Calif.: Addison-Wesley Publishing Co., Inc., 1988.

_____. *Miseducation*. New York: Alfred A. Knopf, 1987.

Fraiberg, Selma. *The Magic Years*. New York: Macmillan Publishing Co., 1959.

Godfrey, Neale S., and Carolina Edwards. *Money Doesn't Grow on Trees*. New York: Simon & Schuster, 1994.

Godfrey, Neale S., and Tad Richards. *A Penny Saved*. New York: Simon & Schuster, 1995.

Greydanus, Donald E., M.D., Editor-in-chief. *Caring for Your Adolescent: Ages 12 to 21*. New York: Bantam Books, 1991.

Keirsey, David, and Marilyn Bates. *Please Understand Me*. Del Mar, Calif.: Prometheus Nemesis Book Co., 1984.

Lazear, David. *Eight Ways of Knowing*. Arlington Heights, Ill.: SkyLight Professional Development, 1999.

Leach, Penelope. *Children First*. New York: Alfred A. Knopf, 1994.

Leman, Kevin. *Making Children Mind Without Losing Yours*. Grand Rapids, Mich.: Baker Book House Co., 1984.

_____. *The New Birth Order Book: Why You Are the Way You Are*. Grand Rapids, Mich.: Baker Book House Co., 1998.

Nelsen, Jane, Ed.D. *Positive Discipline*. New York: Ballantine Books, 1981.

Nelsen, Jane, Cheryl Erwin, and Roslyn Duffy. *Positive Discipline for Preschoolers*. Rocklin, Calif.: Prima Publishing,1995.

Nelsen, Jane, and H. Stephen Glenn. *Raising Self-Reliant Children in a Self-Indulgent World*. Rocklin, Calif.: Prima Publishing & Communications, 1989.

_____. *Time Out*. Fair Oaks, Calif.: Sunrise Press, 1991.

Platt, John M., Ed.D. *Life in the Family Zoo*. Roseville, Calif.: Dynamic Training and Seminars, Inc., 1991.

Bibliography

Popkin, Michael. *Active Parenting*. San Francisco: HarperSanFrancisco, 1987.

Schiff, Donald, M.D., and Steven P. Shelov, M.D., editors. *Guide to Your Child's Symptoms*. New York: Random House, Inc., 1997.

Schor, Edward L., M.D., Editor-in-chief. *Caring for Your School-Age Child: Ages 5 to 12*. New York: Bantam Books, 1995.

Shelov, Steven P., M.D., Editor-in-chief. *Caring for Your Baby and Young Child: Birth to Age 5*. New York: Bantam Books, 1993.

Smith, Hyrum W. *The Power of Time Control*. Audio cassettes of The Famous Franklin Institute Time Management Seminar. Produced by The Franklin Institute, 1986.

Sulloway, Frank J., Ph.D. *Born to Rebel: Birth Order, Family Dynamics, and Creative Lives*. New York: Random House, 1996.

Religious

Covey, Stephen R. *The Seven Habits of Highly Effective Families*. New York: Golden Books, 1997.

Curran, Dolores. *Stress and the Healthy Family*. San Francisco: Harper & Row, Publishers, 1985.

———. *Tired of Arguing with Your Kids?*. Notre Dame: Sorin Books, 1999.

———. *Traits of a Healthy Family*. San Francisco: Harper & Row, Publishers, 1983.

Davidson, James D., et al. *The Search for Common Ground: What Unites and Divides Catholic Americans*. Huntington, Ind.: Our Sunday Visitor, Inc., 1997.

Dobson, James, Ph.D. *On Parenting*. New York: Inspirational Press, 1997.

Eyre, Linda and Richard. *Teaching Your Children Values*. New York: Simon & Schuster, 1993.

Gaither, Gloria, and Shirley Dobson. *Let's Make a Memory: Great Ideas for Building Family Traditions and Togetherness*. Dallas: Word Publishing, 1983.

Heller, David, Ph.D. *Growing up Isn't Hard to Do If You Start out as a Kid*. New York: Random House, 1991.

McCarty, Robert J. *Tips for Raising Teens: A Primer for Parents*. Mahwah, N.J.: Paulist Press, 1998.

Peck, M. Scott, M.D. *The Road Less Traveled*. New York: Simon & Schuster, 1978.

Popcak, Gregory, M.S.W., and Lisa Popcak. *Parenting with Grace*. Huntington: Our Sunday Visitor, Inc., 2000.

Short, Ray. *Sex, Love, or Infatuation: How Can I Really Know?* Minneapolis: Augsburg Publishing House, 1990.

Sonnenberg, Roger. *501 Practical Ways to Love Your Wife and Kids*. St. Louis: Concordia Publishing House, 1996.

Winkler, Kathleen, *How to Risk-Proof Your Kids*. St. Louis: Concordia Publishing House, 1996.

Ziglar, Zig. *Raising Positive Kids in a Negative World*. New York: Thomas Nelson Publishers, 1985.

Books on Special Issues

Death

Fitzgerald, Helen. *The Grieving Child: A Parent's Guide*. New York: Simon & Schuster, 1992.

Grollman, Earl A. *Talking about Death: A Dialogue between Parent and Child*. Boston: Beacon Press, 1990.

Kubler-Ross, Elisabeth. *On Children and Death*. New York: Macmillan Publishing Co., 1983.

Mellonie, Bryan, and Robert Ingpen. *Lifetimes: A Beautiful Way to Explain Death to Children* (a children's book). New York: Bantam Books, 1983.

Schaefer, Dan, and Christine Lyons. *How Do We Tell the Children?: A Step-by-Step Guide for Helping Children Two to Teen Cope When Someone Dies*. New York: Newmarket Press, 1993.

Divorce

Katler, Neil, Ph.D. *Growing up with Divorce: Helping Your Child Avoid Immediate and Later Emotional Problems*. New York: Ballantine Books, 1990.

Hart, Archibald. *Helping Children Survive Divorce: What to Expect; How to Help*. Dallas: Word Publishing, 1996.

Gardner, Richard A., M.D. *The Parents' Book about Divorce*. New York: Bantam Books, 1991.

Sexuality

Ameiss, Bill, and Jane Graver. *Learning about Sex—A Series for the Christian Family: Love, Sex, and God (Ages 14+)*. St. Louis: Concordia Publishing House, 1995.

Bimler, Richard. *Learning about Sex—A Series for the Christian Family: Sex and the New You (Ages 11–14)*. St. Louis: Concordia Publishing House, 1995.

Buth, Lenore. *Learning about Sex—A Series for the Christian Family: How to Talk Confidently with Your Child About Sex*. St. Louis: Concordia Publishing House, 1995.

Graver, Jane. *Learning about Sex—A Series for the Christian Family: How You Are Changing (Ages 8–11)*. St. Louis: Concordia Publishing House, 1995.

Greene, Carol. *Learning about Sex—A Series for the Christian Family: Why Boys and Girls Are Different (Ages 3–5)*. St. Louis: Concordia Publishing House, 1995.

Hummel, Ruth. *Learning about Sex—A Series for the Christian Family:*

Where Do Babies Come From? *(Ages 6–8)* St. Louis: Concordia Publishing House, 1995.

Jones, Stanton L., Ph.D., and Brenna B. Jones. *How and When to Tell Your Kids about Sex: A Lifelong Approach to Shaping Your Child's Sexual Character*. Colorado Springs: NavPress Publishing, 1993.

Pontifical Council for the Family. *The Truth and Meaning of Human Sexuality: Guidelines for Education within the Family*. Washington, D.C.: United States Catholic Conference, 1996.

Sonnenberg, Roger R. *Human Sexuality: A Christian Perspective*. St. Louis: Concordia Publishing House, 1998.

United States Catholic Conference. *Human Sexuality: A Catholic Perspective for Education and Lifelong Learning*. Washington, D.C.: United States Catholic Conference, 1991.

Faith Formation

Barber, Lucie W. *The Religious Education of Preschool Children*. Birmingham: Religious Education Press, 1981.

_____. *Teaching Christian Values*. Birmingham: Religious Education Press, 1984.

Boelhower, Gary J., Ph.D. *Family, Faith, and Fun: Activities, Games, & Prayers for Sharing Faith at Home*. Milwaukee: HI-TIME Publishing Corp., 1996.

Fowler, James W., Ph.D. *Stages of Faith: The Psychology of Human Development and the Quest for Meaning*. San Francisco: Harper Collins Publishers, 1981.

Leslie, Karen. *Faith and Little Children: A Guide for Parents and Teachers*. Mystic, Conn.: Twenty-Third Publications, 1990.

Ratcliff, Donald, ed. *Handbook of Preschool Religious Education*. Birmingham: Religious Education Press, 1988.

Westerhoff, John H., III. *Will Our Children Have Faith?* Harrisburg: Morehouse Publishing, 2000.